How to Create Miracles

IN OUR DAILY LIFE

EDITOR

OSWALD PEREIRA

Vitasta

LET KNOWLEDGE SPREAD

Published by
Renu Kaul Verma
Vitasta Publishing Pvt Ltd
2/15, Ansari Road, Daryaganj,
New Delhi - 110 002
info@vitastapublishing.com

ISBN: 978-93-86473-22-6

First Edition 2018
Second Reprint 2020
MRP ₹ 325

Typeset & Cover Design by Vitasta Publishing Pvt Ltd
Printed by Vikas Computer and Printers

Contents

Dedication *vii*
Contributors *ix*
Editor's Note & Acknowledgements *xv*
Foreword *xix*

BEAUTIFUL WORLD
Beautiful World 3
Why This World is Beautiful 7
The World is One Big Beautiful Family 11
LOVE
The Highest Dharma is Love to All 15
We are all Born With Love and Compassion 18
Your 'Enemy' is a Good Being Like You 21
It Makes Good Sense to Love Your Neighbour 24

Love in Motion 27
Platonic Love is Alive and Kicking 31
The Faith and Love A-Team 35
Love and Compassion: Two True Companions 37
We Live in a World Full of Love 40
GIVING
Seva is True Giving 44
The Joy of Giving 48
Give With Love and Commitment 52
In Giving You Receive 55
Give Silently 58
Give and Grow Rich 61
KARMA
The Best Karma is Love 68
Karma Can be Your Friend 71
You Can Clear Your Karmic Account 75
You are Linked to Your Country's Karma 79
LIFE & LIVING
Neither Success nor Failure Lasts Forever 83
Don't be a Slave to Your Money 87
Relationships and Practical Spirituality 90
Save Your Country From Corruption 93
How to Create Miracles in Our Daily Life 98
The Goal of Married Life 103

Life is a Divine Game 106
Spiritual Ego is Like Excess Baggage 108
Banish Your Ego, Build Your Self-Esteem 111
Namaste! 114
Yoga: A Scientific Philosophy to Transform the World 117

PEACE, HAPPINESS & BLISS

Peace: A Universal Religion 122
We Are Our Own Source of Peace and Happiness 125
Peace and Non-Violence go Hand-in-Hand 128
Spiritual Ideals Spark Happiness 131
Way to Happiness 135
My Quest for Happiness 138
Bliss Vs Happiness 141
A Moment of Bliss 145

POSITIVISM

The Positive Side of Negative Experiences 149
Positivism is to Say Yes to all Good Things 152
Smile a Thousand Times Every Day 156
The Law of Attraction 160

FORGIVENESS

Forgiveness is Divine 165
Forgiveness: A Sweet Gift for Ourselves and Others 168
The Healing Power of Forgiveness 172

Forgive to Take Away the Hurt 175
I Forgave and Was Free 178
GOD & US
Who is Bhagawan? 184
Where is God? 188
How Did We Happen? 193
How I Fell In and Out With God 198
Take a Walk With Divinity 201
Suffering is a Blessing From God 204
Music and Divinity 207
God is Everywhere 210
Beautiful God 213

Dedicated to this beautiful world and its beautiful people.

Contributors

Oswald Pereira: Oswald Pereira, a veteran journalist with more than three decades of experience, is the author of the bestselling and critically acclaimed novels, *The Newsroom Mafia*, *Revenge of the Naked Princess*, *Chaddi Buddies, The Krishna-Christ Connexion, Golmaal In Goa* and *Army Girl Steals Civilian's Heart*. *How to Create Miracles in Our Daily Life* is his first non-fiction book. He is a contributor to *The Speaking Tree* column in *The Times of India*. His spiritual articles have appeared in four *Speaking Tree* anthologies.

Dr Kaity Cama: Dr Kaity Cama has been a healer since childhood. She is a motivational speaker, combining the precepts of practical spirituality with the current trends of marketing strategies. She is a Reiki Grandmaster, graduate of Silva Methods and a qualified clinical hypnotherapist. She is also a freelance writer and photographer.

Rabbi Ezekiel Isaac Malekar: Rabbi Ezekiel Isaac Malekar is an advocate by profession, but devotes his full time to his religious duties. He heals incurable diseases by reciting psalms. A human rights activist, he has participated in more than 2,000 national and international conferences. He has been conferred Doctor of Jewish Welfare, Ambassador of Peace and Mahavir, Mahatma Award for his contribution to inter-faith activities for the last 35 years.

Srila Bhakti Ballabh Tirtha Goswami Maharaj: Srila Bhakti Ballabh Tirtha Goswami Maharaj is President-Acharya of Sree Chaitanya Gaudiya Math since 1979. He is also Founder of GOKUL (Global Organization of Krishna-Chaitanya's Universal Love). For the last 60 years, he has preached the philosophy of Sri Chaitanya Mahaprabhu for universal unity. Since 1997, he has travelled the globe, spreading his message of transcendental divine love. His programmes include dialogues with theologians of all faiths.

Maulana Wahiduddin Khan: Maulana Wahiduddin Khan is an Islamic spiritual scholar who has adopted peace as the mission of his life. Born in Azamgarh in 1925 and known for his Gandhian views, he considers non-violence as the only method to achieve success. Author of more than 200 books, including translation of the Quran in English, Hindi and Urdu, he is also the founder of Centre for Peace and Spirituality International.

Aditya Kumar Choudhary: Aditya Kumar Choudhary, an engineer by profession, says he is a 'regular' guy whom life has taught to keep an open mind, and who learned love and respect from his elders. He does not mind changing and refining his views, aware that sometimes, in the process, views may change as much as say the ore of gold changes to gold.

Reena Singh: Reena Singh, a senior journalist with a spiritual newspaper, has written extensively on service and *seva*, two integral themes in spirituality. "It's great to work in a job where you are paid to do something you really love doing—in my case, imbibing simple ingredients for happier living and editing copy," she says. She's obsessed with the concepts of grammar and editing, which, she thought, drove her existence—till spiritual *gyan*, too, came along her path.

Jeroninio Almeida: Jeroninio 'Jerry' Almeida is a celebrated inspirational orator, motivational speaker, intrepid missionary entrepreneur, firebrand social crusader, teacher, UN advisor, trainer and a renowned, innovative fundraiser. For over a decade, Jerry has been at the forefront to successfully create and execute large format citizen movements like The JOY of GIVING, RIGHT every WRONG, the Karmaveer Awards among others. He is the author of *Karma Kurry: For the Mind, Body, Heart & Soul* and *Karma Kurry for the Hero in Me: Ordinary People Extraordinary Deeds.*

Smita Jayakar: Smita Jayakar, a veteran actress and theatre personality, is also a well-known spiritual healer. Her quest for a deeper understanding of peace and happiness led her to experiment with various natural therapy techniques and practices. After discovering a simple and practical approach to heal her inner self, she shared this with many, helping them heal themselves naturally, through her workshops and tips on holistic healing.

Amar Kumar: Amar Kumar is an internationally known Reiki Master Teacher. He gave up a top corporate job to devote his time to Reiki. He set up Reiki Kendra in 1998 in Kolkata, one of the oldest training and treatment centres in India. He has authored a few books on Reiki and contributes articles to newspapers and magazines.

Juliet Dsouza: Juliet Dsouza says, "A casual nudge from a doctor friend" inspired her to take her first Yoga steps with a personal guru. "The depth and universality of ancient wisdom amazes me. After essential training, I dare to even spread its message, a paradigm shift from the corporate world to the unknown. We must move away from thinking that just tried and tested techniques can heal the world. For over 15 years now, I share my 'light', especially with aspirants to the Catholic priesthood, in an institute in Mumbai."

Yogi Dr Amrit Raj: Yogi Dr Amrit Raj is a fourth generation Ayurvedic doctor and certified 500 Hours Yoga Teacher from Yoga Alliance, USA. He founded Maa Yoga Ashram in Rishikesh, which holds yoga and ayurvedic retreats. He has held yoga and ayurveda workshops for judges, European royal families, Hollywood and Bollywood actors, and UN officials.

Chana Meddin: Chana Meddin discovered Eastern Mysticism after reading the book *Siddhartha* at age 15, which inspired a lifelong commitment to meditation and spirituality. After she began rescuing abused, sick, and dying small animals, she discovered that each embodied the virtues of forgiveness and unconditional love taught by saints. She feels each "Little Buddha" actually rescues her!

Swamini Atmaprajnananda Saraswati: Swamini Atmaprajnananda Saraswati is a Sannyāsini of the Śankara-Bhagavatpāda order. Her published books are *Dasasānti*, *Rupasiddhi*, *Nomenclature of the Vedas*, *Rsikäs of the Rgveda* and *Om: The Sound Symbol*. She is an Advaita Vedantin and Vedic and Sanskrit Scholar, with a PhD in Sanskrit. She disseminates Advaita Vedanta in a simple manner by demystifying it.

Om Swami: Om Swami is a mystic living in the Himalayan foothills. He has a bachelor's degree in business and an MBA from Sydney, Australia. Prior to renunciation, he founded and successfully ran a multinational, multi-million dollar software company. He is the author of *If Truth Be Told: A Monk's Memoir, The Wellness Sense, When All Is Not Well, A Fistful of Love: Wisdom And Humour From A Monk's Bowl, and Kundalini: An Untold Story.*

Arjun Pereira: Arjun Pereira is a singer, musician and guitar teacher. A graduate in mass communication, he has worked as an editor and assistant director with a top production house. His debut short story has appeared in an anthology.

Ismita Tandon: Ismita Tandon is the author of three novels, *Jacob Hills*, *Love Kills* and *Love on the Rocks*. Her poem 'I Am Beautiful' won a prize in the Yahoo-Dove Indibloggers contest. Her latest book is the popular non-fiction title, *OM Swami: As We Know Him*.

Editor's Note & Acknowledgements

How to Create Miracles in Our Daily Life is a first-of-its-kind collection of essays by spiritual gurus and thought leaders on the themes of Love, Life, Living, Giving, Forgiveness, Faith, Compassion, Happiness, Bliss, Peace, Positivism, Karma, and God and Us. Written in simple, crisp language, the tenor of the essays is positive and uplifting; the spiritual teachings are non-didactic and have been demystified. The book has an abundance of tips on practical spirituality that will help readers in day-to-day living.

As the authors are from various faiths, the collection is also a testimony to inter-faith dialogue and to the peaceful coexistence of various religions. It is this inter-faith sharing that makes the book unique and special. The universal message of the book is that this world is beautiful and we are all part of one big family, where the positives are many and completely overshadow the negatives.

My belief in the oneness and beauty of the world inspired me to search for spiritual gurus and thought leaders who share this belief and were willing to contribute their essays for the book.

Compiling and editing the essays for this collection was an enriching experience. I have also contributed essays to the collection. Some of the essays in *How to Create Miracles in Our Daily Life* were chosen from existing works of the authors, while many others were written specially for the collection.

I wish to thank each one of the authors—Srila Bhakti Ballabh Tirtha Goswami Maharaj, Maulana Wahiduddin Khan, Dr Kaity Cama, Om Swami, Swamini Atmaprajnananda Saraswati, Rabbi Ezekiel Isaac Malekar, Smita Jayakar, Amar Kumar, Yogi Dr Amrit Raj, Jeroninio Almeida, Chana Meddin, Ismita Tandon, Juliet Dsouza, Aditya Kumar Choudhary, Arjun Pereira and Reena Singh. Some of Reena's articles first appeared in *The Speaking Tree* newspaper, where she worked as Deputy Editor.

A special thanks to Om Swami for his foreword that sets the tone for this book.

I sincerely thank Renu Kaul Verma, Managing Director of Vitasta Publishing Pvt Ltd, for her support and immense faith in my book. I owe a big thank you to Veena Batra, Editor at Vitasta Publishing for meticulously fine-tuning the manuscript. Team members of Vitasta have worked silently to produce an awesome book. The classic cover conveys the message of the book so well.

My heartfelt thanks to Suhail Mathur, who runs India's fastest growing literary agency, *The Book Bakers*, for finding the right publisher for me.

Behind *How to Create Miracles in Our Daily Life* is the inspiration and blessings of God, whose infinite, unconditional love and divine grace make our world a delightful, beautiful habitat, where we are all one and connected. Thank you, God.

Oswald Pereira

Foreword

OM SWAMI

'Be out in the open to witness the boundless beauty of the world'.

Two friends, a philosopher and a scientist, were camping in the Himalayas. At a high altitude, surrounded by lush mountains, a rejuvenating cool breeze was blowing, caressing them gently. They retired into their shared tent as night began to darken, the flora lending it an ebony beauty beyond expression.

In the middle of the night, the scientist asked the philosopher, "What do you see, my friend?"

"I see infinite beauty around me," the philosopher answered sentimentally. "I hear the waterfalls, I feel the Himalayan air and I see the most magnificent star studded sky. These tiny jewels make me feel as if I'm in the royal court of a world-conqueror, some great emperor. Why, I see heaven. Why do you ask, mate?"

"Someone has stolen our tent, you idiot," the scientist replied.

We are all living in our tents; we are worried about our tents. In our closed boxes, we often fail to see what a beautiful world lies outside. Yes, there are some who will come and try to steal our tents, and some will even succeed in doing so. But, sometimes, that's exactly what's needed to nudge us to step out. To see what a wonder this life is. To witness the boundless beauty of everything that exists in the world, we have to be out in the open.

When I first met Oswald Pereira, I couldn't find a grown-up man in him. Instead, I saw a beautiful child who was eager and willing to help others. There was a childlike curiosity in his eyes, a selfless energy about him. So, when he asked me to write a foreword for his book, *How to Create Miracles in Our Daily Life*, I had no choice but to accept readily and gladly. When I reflected on the contents of the book, I was immediately reminded of the anecdote about the philosopher and the scientist. I thought, here is someone who's trying to remove the covering and urging us to step outside our tent to be a part of this wonderful world.

Oswald has most beautifully collected pearls of wisdom through his own experiences and those of others and threaded them into a priceless necklace in the form of his book. I have no doubt that the readers will enjoy every single part of this book.

Om Swami is a mystic living in the Himalayan foothills. He has a bachelor's degree in business and an MBA from Sydney, Australia. Prior to renunciation, he founded and successfully ran a multinational, multi-million dollar software company. He is the author of *If Truth Be Told: A Monk's Memoir*, *The Wellness Sense*, *When All Is Not Well*, *A Fistful of Love: Wisdom And Humour From A Monk's Bowl*, and *Kundalini: An Untold Story.*

BEAUTIFUL WORLD

Beautiful World

Oswald Pereira

The world is full of lovely, loving, beautiful people. Don't let a miniscule minority of so-called bad persons spoil the party. Let us not shun the party poopers, but invite them instead to join the party.

When we learn to type, we practise with the line, 'Let all good men of the world unite and come to the aid of the party.' Let's make this typing lesson a slogan in our lives.

Positives

If we look at the positives, we will see that the world is a good place to live in. The sun shines every day, the moon lights up the darkness of the night and the stars have been shining forever in the skies. No doubt, we have ups and downs in our lives and we often talk of our bad luck. But if we count our blessings, we will realise how lucky we really are.

Negligible Evil

I don't deny that there is evil around and there are so-called bad persons. But they are in a miniscule minority, barely a fraction of the good people. We often think that the might and power of evil is stronger than the good. That happens when we cloud our outlook with negativity. But it is in the law of nature that good always triumphs over evil in the end. You just need to have faith in yourself, your near and dear ones and the world around you.

Loving Neighbours

We complain about our neighbours. But if we do a reality check, we will soon realise that we have more neighbours who love us than those who hate us. Loving and giving begins at home. When we love and give enough at home, then we can extend that love and giving to our neighbours. And rest assured, your neighbours will reciprocate in equal measure, if not more, sooner than later.

True Givers

We've seen enough proof of the truly giving nature of people around us during many natural calamities like earthquakes and floods. There are many true givers who are more keen to give than to receive. Believe me when I say that there is great joy in giving. It is an opportunity given to us to share not only our material possessions, but more importantly, love and knowledge. When God gives, he doesn't ask us for anything in return. So, when we give, we should not expect anything in return. We don't go to heaven by giving, but if we all learn to give, this earth could seem like a heaven.

Happiness and Bliss

In the *Bhagavad Gita*, Krishna tells Arjuna that no man can know happiness without peace. But to experience peace, we need to prepare ourselves to receive it. So it is we who are responsible for peace and happiness in our life. Once we realise this, peace and happiness will flow in our lives like a never-ending spring, making us jump with joy. The famous poet John Milton said, "The mind is its own place, and in itself can make a heaven of hell, a hell of heaven." This is, however, an incomplete truth. The real and complete truth is that it is the spirit that rules the mind. With a spirit full of love, optimism and calmness, heaven is a feeling that is within us all the time. The right word is, perhaps, bliss.

Love, Forgiveness and Happiness

When we love ourselves, it becomes easier to love others; and to forgive them if they have done us any harm. Pure happiness is achieved when you forgive a person, because you then detoxify yourself of all negative energy, free your mind and purify your soul and body. Love, forgiveness and happiness is a triple bounty bestowed on us. These are qualities that help us to transcend our humanness and get closer to divinity.

Boundless Grace and Goodness

As so much of positive energy, love, compassion and kindness surrounds us, don't you think that the world is a place with boundless grace and goodness—a world that gives us great cause for celebration? But it is a celebration that never ends, because grace and goodness are not like a piece of cake that is eaten, digested and forgotten. Grace and goodness can't be measured in quantities. These are infinite and inexhaustible attributes that no power on earth can destroy.

God's Blessings

Behind all the beauty and goodness is God's blessings. The Supreme Being has blessed us with Divine Grace and showers us with unconditional love. God is here, there and everywhere…in all things big and small. Every moment that we live is a blessing from God. Every drop of water that we drink is a gift from God. As poet Kabir says, we can find God in the "tiniest house of time...God is the breath inside the breath."

Why This World is Beautiful

Dr Kaity Cama

When Shakespeare said that all the world is a stage and all men and women are actors, did he understand the truth and profundity of his own words? For indeed this world is a stage where we are all performing in different roles.

At subtler levels, we know that though we are here in this world, we are not really of this world. Every religion has always told us this truth.

As spiritual beings, then, without form or substance or gender, how do we experience what we call material life? How can we inhale the heady fragrances of flowers? How can we feel the texture of the desert sands? How can we enjoy sunshine, rain, the changing seasons? How can we experience companionship and interactions when in the spiritual realm we are all one? And we received this divine gift, this marvellous human body with physical senses.

The Creator, with unconditional love, gifted us the means to experience the world of matter, to experience companionship and interactions. That, by itself, is a miracle. Even today, scientists cannot explain how from a single cell there emerge billions of cells of different types and they are unable to duplicate the manufacture of a single human body.

Then there is the earth itself. What infinite intelligence holds it in place, orbiting around the sun? There is constant creation going on in nature. Every few years, scientists discover yet another new planet.

The miracle is that this seemingly reassuring material world is just fluctuations of intelligence and energy, stuff which is invisible to the human eye, and yet through the marvel of our brain and nervous system (which again are fluctuations of intelligence and energy), we are able to perceive it through the physical senses. And so, with the divine gift of a human body, we experience these fluctuations of intelligence and energy as 'matter'.

At higher states of consciousness, we do perceive this world as a stage with all of us acting out roles. And even though through our personality we change our original 'script', it is a superb experience.

If we study the evolution of mankind, we discover through our intellect how far we have evolved as humans. Of course, we still need to evolve spiritually, because we got so interested in material life that we put aside the soul's original desire, but thankfully now, more and more humans are turning back to spirituality.

This world is a beautiful place because we learn about relationships and interactions with others. In fact, it would be no exaggeration to say that this world is a place of relationships... relationships between human and human, relationships between corporate and corporate, relationships between countries. And just look at the relationship within the human body itself—how everything is really interlinked.

Let's also look at the relationship of the mind with the body, of the body to this earth and to the universe. Everyone and everything is connected. There is nothing that is isolated in the world. We are citizens not merely of a country, but of the universe itself.

Those of us who are too deeply immersed in material life may argue that the world is full of conflicts and disturbing factors. And those of us who see the bigger picture will respond that conflicts and disturbing factors are not caused by the world, only by those who have yet to evolve to higher consciousness, where everyone sees everyone else as their own self, where the realization comes that 'hurting you is hurting my own self', where we know there is no 'separateness', all are just one. For every conflict, every hurt, there are at least hundred acts of kindness in the world.

Beauty is as beauty sees. When we seek the beautiful in people, it really does show itself and this world becomes a miraculous, glorious experience for us.

We arrived here with nothing and we will leave here with nothing to take back to our spiritual abode. As long as we remember this, we will balance our earthly life with spirituality and then be able to see with gratitude in our heart, how very, very beautiful this world really is.

The World is One Big Beautiful Family

Rabbi Ezekiel Isaac Malekar

God created the world and mankind. There is but one creator and one human species. So doesn't it follow that we are all part of one big universal world family?

If we firmly believe in one God of all creation and mankind, then it would be logical to conclude that the world is united, bound together by mutual love. To put it succinctly, the Universal Creator is one and so is mankind—one and united. The scriptures say: "Behold how good and how pleasant it is for brothers to dwell together in unity. Unity is the very essence of the Creative Being."

Let us all say the following prayer so that brotherhood and unity prevail on this planet:

"We have learnt in recent years how to fly through the air like birds and how to swim under the ocean like fish. Teach us, O, God! how to walk the earth like men in brotherhood and the dignity to live together, to work together and to share together life's experiences for ourselves and our children. Amen."

It may seem difficult for us to live together, considering that each one of us has special desires, beliefs and attitudes. In a family, a society, or a city, a state, and the world, at large, different people have different views and tastes. But there is one way by which we can live together—by trying to blur the differences between us. It is said that religion divides people and breaks the unity of mankind. But this is not what religion and its practice does if we follow its spirit.

The practice of religion must be closely integrated with daily living. Our every action must bear in mind that the Almighty is watching us with loving kindness. Goodness and religion go hand-in-hand. If we separate goodness from religion or religion from goodness, then it is tantamount to keeping God out of our everyday life. Religion is a way of life—a daily practice. Religion is not like wealth that we acquire and preserve in a safe deposit box. Religion is not a commodity to be placed in a freezer to be defrosted for use. Religion must be used constantly to be of significance and to make a difference to us and mankind.

Religion is based on peace, universal brotherhood, tolerance, mutual respect, compassion, self-sacrificial love, harmony and unity. There is absolutely no room for hatred or violence in religion, even if somebody hurts your religious sentiments.

In the words of Mahatma Gandhi: "My religion is based on Truth and non-violence. Truth is my God and non-violence is a means of realising Him. All religions are true and equal. Humanity is the only true religion."

Perhaps, the best way to sum up the unity of mankind is with the Sanskrit phrase, *Vasudhaiva Kutumbakam*—'The world is one family'.

As a *shloka* (believed to be from the Vedas) says: "We are birds of the same nest. We may wear different skins. We may speak different languages. We may believe in different religions. We may belong to different cultures. Yet we share the same home, our Earth. We are born on the same planet, covered by the same skies, gaze at the same stars, breathe the same air. We must learn to progress together, or miserably perish together. For, a person can live individually, but can only survive collectively."

Beautiful words that go to show what a beautiful world we live in.

LOVE

The Highest Dharma is Love to All

Srila Bhakti Ballabh Tirtha Goswami Maharaj

What is dharma? Dharma means that which holds the individual, family, society, country, the whole world, together. Where there is dharma, there can be no conflict. For dharma enables a way of life that ensures peace and harmony, truth and justice.

When the path of dharma is abandoned, you find yourself following adharma, which is just the opposite.

Dharma has various aspects to it. One is *brahmacharya* or celibacy. Second, *satya*, truth. When you speak untruth or are dishonest in your actions, it will hurt you, your family, society and country. Untruthfulness is adharma that could disturb the whole world. Misguiding people, getting involved in scams and cheating are all acts of adharma.

The third limb of dharma is *tapasya* or penance, when you withdraw your senses from all objects of sensual pleasure. While performing penance, do you inflict injury on anybody in this world? We commit all kinds of sins for sense gratification. *Tapasya* helps you to stay in control.

The fourth characteristic of dharma is charity. Whatever you earn, if you use only for yourself and do not give to anyone else including family members, this is adharma. Without parents would one survive in this world? Everyone is indebted to them. They have a right over your income. If one does not give them any money, then it is adharma.

Every adharma has a reaction. One takes the help of other human beings and the natural world. They give us so much. We must pay them back. If we don't return their goodness, then it is adharma. One must give charity or contribute in some way. Dharma cannot bring violence; it ushers in only peace. Sinful acts and reactions are due to adharma.

The fifth constituent of dharma is *niyam*, which means following a regulated life. If you do not observe regulation of body, you might become vulnerable to disease. Regulation of mind, institutions and society is essential. Discipline is necessary. This is dharma. One follows rules for enhancement of body, mind and intellect, following the examples and teachings of experienced guides.

The sixth aspect of dharma is forgiveness, so necessary to live harmoniously in a family, society or country. Anybody can make mistakes knowingly or unknowingly. You need to forgive people to maintain harmony in society and build bridges of friendship and love.

The seventh feature of dharma is non-violence. If you inflict injury on another, there is bound to be a reaction. For every action there is a reaction. Do not use any force, for there will be a reaction. Violence of any kind ignites more violence.

The eighth aspect of dharma is tranquillity of mind. If the mind is disturbed, you cannot take a proper decision. All good decisions are taken with a calm mind. When we are obsessed with worldly matters, we are more likely to be angry and disturbed, always.

Whenever we get angry and disturbed, we are likely to disturb and harm others in return. But whenever we meditate on the most tranquil entity, the Supreme Being, our mind becomes calm and serene, and then we can take the right decisions.

The ninth limb of dharma is austerity. All these aspects of dharma will in no way harm anyone. Indeed, following dharma will improve our quality of life.

There are different levels of dharma.

But the highest dharma is to love all.

To attain this is to be blessed with actual philosophical knowledge. But this peak will be scaled only by those who have actual realisation.

We are all Born With Love and Compassion

Maulana Wahiduddin Khan

There is a well-known saying attributed to Jesus Christ: "Love your enemy." *(Matthew)* This saying holds highest importance for fostering love. Love includes compassion, as both love and compassion are synonymous with each other. 'Love your enemy' means love everyone including your enemy.

The love culture is common to all religions. Raja Mahendra Pratap Singh wrote a book in 1917 with the title, *Religion of Love*. In this book, he rightly argues that love is the essential spirit of all religions. It can be said that religion is love and love is religion.

The same is true for the religion of Islam. Here, I would like to refer to a verse from the *Quran*. "Good and evil deeds are not equal. Repel evil with what is better; then you will see that one who was once your enemy has become your dearest friend." (41:34)

In this verse, the *Quran* refers to a law of nature. Everyone is born with the spirit of love and compassion. No one is devoid of this spirit. When everyone is born with love, it means that love is the rule and enmity is an exception. If you experience enmity from a person, you should not take it seriously. Rather, take it as a temporary deviation from his nature, and it would be quite possible to make him return to his original nature based on love.

If you avoid the culture of reaction, you will acquire a new strength—that of making a friend out of an enemy. According to nature, human society is a society of love. In other words, every enemy is your potential friend.

You have to turn this potential into actual. What is required on our part is simple adherence to one principle: Don't react, but rather try to live with good behaviour even among those who resort to misbehaviour. If you adopt this attitude, a miracle will occur: your enemy will become your dearest friend.

Love and compassion are not just mere words of the dictionary. Almost every home has a living manifestation of these qualities, that is, persons with whom you have blood relationship. What is a family? Family is a small unit of society.

In society, relationships are established on the basis of neighbourhood. In a family, relationships are established on the basis of blood relationship. Blood relation is a very strong factor for love. This is the reason why we see the love culture in every family. A family is a mini society, which gives us a lesson on how to live in the greater society with love.

If in society, people live with others just as they live with blood relatives in their family, then certainly a society will emerge in which values of love and compassion will prevail. Take your family as a teacher and you will certainly be able to become a good member of your society. Love is not a unilateral culture; rather it is a bilateral culture.

When you love others, you create an atmosphere in which the other person will also respond to you with love. Consumer items can be acquired from shopping centres, but there is only one way to get good members for society, and that is, to live by the ethics based on love and compassion.

It is this culture that is called Sufi culture. One Persian Sufi saint has given this definition for Sufi culture: "*Ma qissa-e-sikandar wa dara na khanda aim. As ma bajuz hiqayat-e-mehr wa wafa mapurs.*" (We don't know the story of kings and emperors. We know only the story of love and compassion.)

Your 'Enemy' is a Good Being Like You

Oswald Pereira

"Patrick, you should hate alcohol; it's your worst enemy," exclaims the village priest, Father John, as he sees Patrick staggering out of a tavern.

"But Father, doesn't Jesus say that we must love our enemies?" quips Patrick.

"Jesus asked us to love our enemies, but he never meant we should drink them up," Father John says, smiling.

But it isn't really funny, because the joke could be on you. When you hate your enemy, it does more harm to you and your health than to your so-called enemy.

Hatred, resentment, enmity and anger lead to hypertension, heart ailments, ulcers and more.

Nelson Mandela points out that resentment is like drinking poison and then hoping it will kill your enemies. To make peace with your enemy, you have to work with him; then he becomes your partner, adds Mandela.

"There's something about love that builds up and is creative. There is something about hate that tears down and is destructive. So love your enemies," said Martin Luther King Jr.

Before you indulge yourself in unbridled hate for your enemies, understand why you have reached rock bottom in your relationships. Ask yourself why you have so many enemies. Is it the fault of your enemies or are you the one to blame?

In the *Bhagavad Gita*, Krishna says, "One who is equal to friends and enemies, who is equipoised in honour and dishonour, heat and cold, happiness and distress, fame and infamy, who is always free from contaminating association, always silent and satisfied with anything, who doesn't care for any residence, who is fixed in knowledge and who is engaged in devotional service—such a person is very dear to Me."

Just think. If only we did some introspection, we would realise that our enemies are a creation of our mind that is full of ego, envy, anger, resentment, bitterness and hatred. And the result? The result is nothing but a world full of enemies. It's like a prison we have created for ourselves.

When Mandela was released from prison after 27 years, he said, "As I walked out the door toward the gate that would lead to my freedom, I knew that if I didn't leave my bitterness and hatred behind, I'd still be in prison."

To come back to the *Gita*, Krishna says, "One who is not envious but is a kind friend to all living entities, who doesn't think himself a proprietor and is free from false ego, who is equal in both happiness and distress, who is tolerant, always satisfied, self-controlled, and engaged in devotional service with determination, his mind and intelligence fixed on Me—such a devotee of Mine is very dear to Me."

When you understand that you are capable of earning God's love, then you'll love yourself; from this state of mind will spring love for all beings. Then you'll see that it is not in your nature to hate.

You'll realise the person whom you believe is your enemy is really a good being like you, deserving your kindness, friendship, and love. So why not make the effort to love your so-called enemy?

It Makes Good Sense to Love Your Neighbour

Oswald Pereira

Why should I love my neighbour like I love myself? The answer is simple: Because it's the most sensible thing to do.

Loving your neighbour is the first and best choice among the three choices you have. The first choice is love. The second is hate and the third is indifference.

Let's examine each choice, beginning with the third choice. Perhaps, you don't want to love your neighbour, because he is bad; but yet you wouldn't want to hate him because you are a good person and you avoid negative emotions. So you are indifferent to your neighbour.

But indifference or apathy is a cold emotion. Apathy is as negative as hatred. The line between hatred and apathy is very fine. If you meet your neighbour on the street and you ignore him, it's hardly a good and decent thing to do.

The second choice—hatred—will harm you as much

as it hurts your neighbour...which leaves you with the first and the best choice—to love your neigbhour.

Honestly, loving an irksome neighbour is not as hard as it seems. It simply means respecting the person and thinking of his needs and desires as much as you would your own. You won't be able to love yourself until you first love your neighbour.

Whether we like it or not, a major part of our life will always centre on that of our neighbours. Ask yourself some questions and you'll see from the answers how important your neighbour is for your own peace and happiness. And you can't just stop at loving your immediate neighbour. You've got to love your neighbour's neighbour too and your neighbour's neighbour's neighbour and...the circle of love gets wider subsuming differences of community, state, nation, continents—encompassing the whole universe and beyond.

Your heart is so big and so full of love, that its capacity to love is infinite; it's Divine. Inversely, your heart's capacity to hate is limited. Try applying the Golden Rule of infinite love to hate and you'll find yourself shattered. That's because you don't have a limitless capacity to hate like you have to love. For, love gives you joy and power and victory and hate brings in sorrow and powerlessness and defeat.

Different religions propound love of your neighbour as an important part of their teaching. But you don't have to be a religious person to love your neighbour...because love of your neighbour is a superb human emotion, not necessarily tied to any creed or religion.

"Love the Lord your God with all your heart and with all your soul and with all your mind." This is the first and greatest teaching. And the second greatest teaching is: "Love your neighbour as yourself." All other teachings hinge on these two teachings. This is how Christianity explains the Golden Rule of 'Love Thy Neighbour.'

World religions have strikingly like-minded beliefs on the Golden Rule. Hindus believe that one should never do to others what would pain oneself; Islam says not one of you is a believer until he loves for his brother what he loves for himself. The Sikh faith asks you to treat others as you would like to be treated. That nature is only good when it shall not do unto another whatever is not good for its own self is a precept of the Zoroastrian faith. Buddhists say, hurt not others with that which pains yourself. And Confucius said: "Do not do to others what you do not want them to do to you."

Love in Motion

Dr Kaity Cama

Three little words which activate the music of the Universal spheres in the human heart, mind and soul are, "I love you."

Sometimes they are felt as emotions, sometimes as inspirations to soar higher spiritually, and sometimes they are spoken without any attachment or feeling whatsoever, carelessly uttered almost as a duty.

What *is* love really? When asked this question, different individuals respond differently. To some it is the feeling of closeness to their beloved one—a husband, a wife, a partner; to some others, it is an emotion of perhaps overwhelming gratitude when something nice is done for them by another. Earthly or this-world love may truly be an emotion, yes, but the real meaning of love is something much more profound, much deeper than this-world reality could suggest. It is the experience of the oneness of the entire Universe and Creation.

Even though the everyday person may not have reached the level of experiencing that oneness, let us look at the mundane situations where the "I love you" is being said with emotion. Let us take as an example, a husband-and-wife situation. Each says these words regularly to the other, which is beautiful. Now comes the test of love. A mother-in-law comes for an extended visit to their home.

Perhaps the husband does not really enjoy the anticipated visit, because subconsciously he knows it is going to upset his routine in the sense that of course his wife would spend time with her mother.

So, during his mother-in-law's visit, the husband becomes a bit grumpy, a bit irritated, a bit aloof from his wife. This type of situation crops up ever so often in the lives of couples. During such times, where has the love gone? If we think about love between couples, we need to think of a two-way street—of support—emotional support, of sharing each other's troubles as well as joys.

If having her mother with her for say three months makes his wife happy, then he should also be feeling happy because if he truly loves his wife as he says he does, then her happiness should be paramount to him.

The same goes for the wife when her husband's mother or father or relatives come to visit. These are real-life situations, which often cause so much conflict between couples that finally the "I love you" ends up in a divorce court.

Love in motion is, on this planet, to be helpful, supportive, sharing, and understanding with one's dear ones. The simplest way to do this is to take a bit of time to think: "If our roles were reversed, how would I want my spouse to be with me? In what way would it make me feel happier?" If we are willing to think honestly and truly about this, our attitude would change dramatically, actually putting love in motion.

Sometimes, one unfortunate incident takes root in a spouse's mind, even though it may have occurred several years ago, and the negative splinter is almost deliberately not removed. Why not? Because of ego's prompting: "Remember what happened?"

Unfortunately, we do not remember the good things, the happier things that took place, but we hold this negative splinter within us, thinking of the other individual as an enemy when he/she could be a very good and trustworthy friend. Most of us do this sort of thing on a regular basis almost.

Five years ago, perhaps someone said something that was not intended the way we perceived it to be, but we chose, actually chose to hold on to that, forgetting what our part in the incident was! Reality is created within us, that is a fact.

Someone who may be in really constant and excruciating physical pain and who is trying his/her level best to be cheerful and not burden others with that expression of pain is sometimes called 'haughty', or some such adjective. The reality we perceive as 'haughtiness' or 'superiority' is created within us through our own perceptions, whereas the true reality is something quite different.

Love in motion means compassion, and we all do have compassion, do we not? Love in motion means service to others, and we are all capable of that, are we not? Love in motion means putting our own desires and needs on hold for a while and concentrating instead on acts of genuine kindness.

Remember that the spark of Divinity which is within us is within the other individual too. Those individuals who actually put love in motion are doing something extraordinarily remarkable—they are, without even being aware of it, channels of Divine blessings to others.

Platonic Love is Alive and Kicking

Oswald Pereira

Can there be close bonding, without any physical attraction between a man and a woman?

'I have a close friend of the opposite sex—someone I have known for ten years, since I was sixteen years old. We have a very nurturing relationship and there has never been a hint of sexual attraction between us. I am married now, and my new family, especially my husband, views this relationship with suspicion. I have been told to stop meeting or talking to my friend. How can I make them understand that this is purely platonic? That you can love a man just as you love a girlfriend, a cousin, or even a brother or sister'—Kavita Bajaj (name changed).

This kind of situation is pretty common, especially among those who live in urban areas where there are less restrictions on socialising with members of the opposite sex. The question that comes to mind is how many of us interpret platonic love correctly?

If her husband had a similar platonic relationship, would Kavita have accepted it? Often a spouse tends to use the term 'platonic' to put the partner off the scent of infidelity. And in Kavita's case, she is wrong in comparing platonic love to the love for a girlfriend, a cousin or a sibling.

Platonic love is much more than mere friendship between two girls, two boys or a boy and a girl. It is definitely different from filial love or the love between a brother and sister or cousins. And a *rakhi*-brother that a girl may adopt is not a platonic lover.

Platonic love is always between the opposite sexes; it's not a flirtatious fling that we are talking about, but a strong commitment of mutual love and respect; very spiritual, bordering on the divine. You love the heart, mind and soul, and not the physical appearance.

However, there's always the lurking danger of sensuality souring a platonic relationship. And it takes just one indiscreet moment to erase the *Lakshman Rekha* of 'no sex please' between two platonic lovers.

Interestingly, platonic love in its original form had nothing to do with gender. The concept of platonic love arose in Plato's *Symposium* and *Phaedrus*. It was love meant to bring two lovers closer to wisdom and the Platonic form of beauty.

The examples given by Plato refer exclusively to the love between a man and a boy. By the mid-18th century, platonic friendship and platonic love were commonly used to signify an intense but sexless relationship between two members of the opposite sex.

However, when we study recent Indian history, doubts crop up whether platonic love can really exist. Do you believe that Pandit Jawaharlal Nehru's love for Edwina Mountbatten was platonic? Do you think that Mohandas Karamchand Gandhi's close relationships with more than a dozen women were platonic?

Various commentators have raised doubts on the platonic nature of Nehru's relationship with Edwina. However, Edwina's daughter, Pamela Mountbatten has said in her book, *India Remembered: A Personal Account of the Mountbattens During the Transfer of Power*, that while "love blossomed between the 'lonely' widowed prime minister and her British socialite mother, the relationship was purely platonic."

However, in chats with half-a-dozen odd friends from age groups ranging between twenty and sixty, I get the distinct impression that platonic love is alive and kicking. Says advertising guru, poet and singer, Cedric Serpes: "Platonic interdependency is possible. Sex is by no means a yardstick to measure love."

Adds physician Jitu Rajgor, "Platonic love is possible

and it exists." But he clarified: "Mostly, it is one-sided."

Rupa Gulab, author of four novels, says that platonic love is possible "so long as both individuals in the relationship have low sex drives. Also, as couples grow older together, love does tend to become more platonic than physical," she adds.

That's a view also endorsed by development consultant Kiran Negi who says that many couples after some years of marriage are more like "companions and soul mates."

Army wife, Priya Khanna believes that platonic relationships "resonate the Indian way of life, which believes in the purity of man-woman union."

Payal Gwalani, a young communications specialist says she is connected spiritually with her platonic soulmate who is ten years her senior.

And when she gets married, he will continue to be a part of her life. But she'll make sure that the man she marries 'is understanding' enough to accept this. Good luck, Payal!

The Faith and Love A-Team

Oswald Pereira

It is said that faith can move mountains. But what good would we achieve by a feat like moving mountains?

Wouldn't it be better if faith can move the world to love... and end all manner of injustice and hatred?

Love and faith, in fact, are intertwined with each other. You love a person only if you have faith in her/him. And your faith is strengthened as love grows for that person.

What brings you closer to God—love or faith? A confusing question, it would seem, at first. But when we ponder a bit, we may come to the conclusion that the two are interlinked. For, to love God, we need to have faith in Him. And it is our faith that builds our love for Him.

To put the question differently, does love inspire faith or does faith inspire love? Sounds like the tricky chicken and egg dilemma. What comes first, faith or love?

Like there can be no egg without a chicken and no chicken without an egg, it may seem that there can be no faith without love and no love without faith.

Christians chant an *Act of Faith* prayer and an *Act of Love* prayer as well. The first affirms, 'O my God, I firmly believe that you are one God in three divine persons.' The second reiterates, 'O My God, I love you above all things, with my whole heart and soul, because you are all good and worthy of all love.'

The two prayers clearly show that faith and love are, indeed, connected and feed on each other, so to say.

The *Bhagavad Gita* says *Bhakti* is the love for God and love reinforced by a true knowledge of the glory of God. It surpasses the love for all things worldly.

All that God wants is love, faith, assurance that you are a pure devotee and that your love for Him is not measured in terms of your riches or position in life.

'If one offers Me with love and devotion a leaf, a flower, fruit or water, I will accept it,' says Lord Krishna. These divine words further establish the connection between faith or devotion and love (for God).

So, since faith and love are intertwined, let us pray that faith and love join hands and form an A-Team to mow down mountains of hate and anger and build a universe full of hope, justice and love.

Love and Compassion: Two True Companions

Oswald Pereira

Love and compassion are the core of all religions. When teamed together, love and compassion bind the body and mind with the soul.

But just like we need to love ourselves first to love others, compassion springs only when we start looking at ourselves with compassion and understanding, accepting and loving ourselves as we are.

One may travel the whole world in search of one who is more worthy of compassion than oneself, and yet not find that person, the Buddha said. So true. But love and compassion are truly faithful companions that nurture each other. Simply expressed, compassion is to feel the pain and suffering of another person so much that one makes it one's own and does everything to end it. However, it is love that moves one to compassion, or alternatively, compassion that sparks love for all living beings.

Compassion 'supplies the complement' to loving kindness, according to the American monk, Bhikkhu Bodhi. Imbued with loving kindness, we work towards the happiness of others. And when we are compassionate, we explore how we can make all living beings free from suffering.

Love, compassion and happiness, work for the receiver as well as the giver. As the current Dalai Lama (XIV), says: "If you want others to be happy, practice compassion. If you want to be happy, practice compassion."

In Hinduism too, compassion is known by several words such as *daya*, *karuna*, *anukampa*, and *anukrosha*. It is considered one of the necessary paths to being happy. Compassion has been described as a virtue that treats a stranger, a relative, a friend and a foe, indeed all living beings as one's own self, desiring their welfare and good. Compassion is not pity because that would mean condescension; it is truly feeling that everyone's suffering is one's own suffering.

In Judaism, God is invoked as the Father of Compassion. Thus, *Rahmana* or Compassionate is regarded as His revealed word.

The *Quran* emphasises *Rahman* and *Rahim*, mercy and compassion. Each of the 114 chapters of the *Quran*, with one exception, begins with the verse, "In the name of Allah the Compassionate, the Merciful."

In the *Bible* too, God is spoken of as the "Father of

compassion" and the "God of all comfort." Christianity is founded on love and compassion. Jesus Christ, whom Christians believe is the Son of God, epitomised love and compassion. Compassion is that which makes the heart of the good move at the pain of others, says the Buddha. It crushes and destroys the pain of others and shelters and embraces the distressed. Buddha told his personal attendant, Ananda, "the cultivation of loving kindness and compassion is all of our practice."

Compassion for all life, human and non-human, is central to Jainism. Jain monks go to all lengths to avoid killing any living creature, wearing a face mask to avoid inhaling the smallest fly and walking barefoot.

So since love and compassion are central to every religion, does this mean that non-believers in religion are devoid of these noble virtues? Not at all.

As the Dalai Lama points out: "Compassion is not religious business, it is human business; it is not luxury; it is essential for our own peace and mental stability; it is essential for human survival." Then he goes on to say, "Love and compassion are the true religions to me. But to develop these, we do not need to believe in any religion," he concludes.

We Live in a World Full of Love

Aditya Kumar Choudhary

So much has been written about love by writers, poets and philosophers. All religions, unequivocally, propagate the message of love.

But it is the sixth century BC mystic philosopher, Lao Tzu (also called Lao Tse and known by several other names), whose thoughts on love seem so complete and comprehensive. Lao Tzu, the founder of Taoism, showed how faith, justice, power, knowledge and other good and great things in life would be so meaningless without love. If love makes the world go round and run well, its absence leads to desolation and emptiness. As Lao Tzu said, 'Faith without love breeds fanaticism; truth without love stirs criticism; knowledge without love feeds dogmatism.' What's the use of power if not coupled with love? For power without love leads to violence, and to despotism in the worst case scenario.

Justice and honour, duty and worthiness, education and order make for a good, modern, civil society. But Lao Tzu told the world 2,600 years ago that justice without love would generate hardness and honour without love cultivates pride; duty without love spells annoyance; worthiness without love spurs arrogance; education without love causes contradiction; and order without love instigates pettiness and, worse, chaos—all this is the very antithesis of a civilised society. Taking a cue from the wise mystic, one could add that life itself is meaningless without love. Then it becomes a life of lifelessness. Add love to life and see the turnaround—see how the world becomes a lively place worth living.

Now add love to duty and you produce that nice thought of devotion; couple truth with love and it springs forth compassion; worthiness matched with love creates humbleness; education with love germinates wisdom; justice joined with love nurtures reform and transformation. Order when accompanied by love breeds harmony; knowledge with love brings forth understanding.

When power and love walk hand-in-hand, the happy outcome is great leadership. Honour with love cultivates gratitude; and faith with love gives rise to the world's greatest spiritualists and the most humane religions.

Love can bring pain too; but that very pain is part of

the learning curve that propels you to finer, higher levels of love. In times of disaster and natural calamities, it's love which sustains us together, as was demonstrated by the people of Japan and the world standing by their side. In Mumbai, during the deluge of 26 July, 2005, when hundreds of lives were lost and scores of people were stranded, and the administration and governance came to a standstill, it was human love that came to the rescue when strangers helped strangers. It was a true example of one big family or *vasudhaiva kutumbakam*.

We, as humans, should not only love ourselves, our parents, our near and dear ones, and friends but even total strangers as well as our enemies. Our love should extend to mother earth, the plant and animal kingdom; the whole of God's beautiful creation.

The youth of today are struggling to find out what love is. Infatuation and lust is made out to be love. Love is said to be the gate to bliss, which is, in effect, God; and the experience of the Divine Grace of the Supreme Being.

God's love is unconditional.

Love has an infinite energy; the more you give, the more you receive; the older love grows, the greater is its power to elevate you to supreme joy and glory.

It is believed that the last stanzas of the *Upanishads* are still to be written. I hope and I pray that the last word in the completed *Upanishads* will be love.

GIVING

Seva is True Giving

Reena Singh

Do you give your money away in the spirit of *seva*? Or do you constantly think of where your money goes—whether it really reaches the needy? When you give, you do get a high, even if you gave from a selfish motive, including in order to feel good about yourself.

Whatever the motive—by giving, you are helping another who is less fortunate; you think, perhaps, it is a prudent way to give away some excess money that you have so that you earn good *karma* and save on taxes—a double blessing.

When you give and another receives, you feel useful. On the other hand, doubts can, and they do assail every bone in your body. Can you really afford to give away your hard-earned money, you ask yourself. Will your money really reach the needy? What if someone undeserving and greedy gets hold of your donation? What if a part of what you give away in all earnestness, goes into pleasure-seeking, immoral activities by the end beneficiary?

There is another simple disconnect, that tiny, yet nagging voice that tells you that when tithing or the spiritual practice of giving away a part of your income for charity was a way of life, it was in another era altogether, when governments perhaps didn't impose swinging taxes, eroding your savings plan.

Taxes are anyway meant to go into infrastructure development for all, besides public, charitable programmes such as education and healthcare for everyone, so must you 'tax' yourself further by giving to charity as well?

The author of *Freakonomics*, Stephen J Dubner says, "pretend for a moment that you are in the 40 per cent tax bracket; don't you ever find yourself thinking, 'Hey, I already donate so much of my income to various causes that have little to do with my personal well-being, so why should I give a penny more to 'charity'?"

In other words, how much of your 'annual', feel-good, Rs 5,000 giveaway to charity actually reaches that little boy or girl whose image you recall from that particular charity's glossy brochure? What if your contribution is inadvertently siphoned off to fund invisible perks allocated to the head honcho and his assistants who run the NGO you volunteer to support?

People handling your money may have good intentions, but is everyone on that team honest? Didn't a government functionary cite research that out of every rupee the government collects from you, in the form of taxes or donations, just 16 paise actually reaches the target populace in the form of services?

If so, what happens to the rest? It is 'lost in transit', a glib government might offer by way of explanation. That is, your hard-earned money ends up lining the coffers of unscrupulous people, of people on 'committees', and on those who go on fact-finding missions and embark on likely unproductive study programmes to examine the problem at hand.

Of course, the one simple way to get over this would be to be more pro-active in the charity or NGO you are endorsing. Also, forget about the tax you are saving. Give anonymously and give it sincerely. Want to help people survive the cold? Give blankets away to the local slum dwellers near your house. Feed the poor—give them vegetables, dal, flour and fruits, even if you can't cook the food yourself.

Want to donate to a school, but don't wish to give money for you think it will end up in someone's pocket? Go out and give students notebooks instead, or pens, pencils and erasers, or buy sets of books for students who can't afford to buy them.

Get personally involved and you will see and know where your money is going, where it will make a difference.

It's even better if you actually volunteer some of your time. Give of yourself, unconditionally, with no expectation of recognition or certification.

This, perhaps, is true *seva*.

The Joy of Giving

Jeroninio Almeida

Giving is to try and encourage a mindset change at a mass level, where there is social justice, fairness and equality for all. It is not mindless, arrogant charity but humble, inclusive social justice that is wanting in our world. Why do we say mindless arrogant charity vs humble, inclusive social justice? As the Islamic prophet Imam Ali said, "What are human beings so arrogant about? Our origin is a sperm, our end is a carcass and in between we are a vessel for excrement."

This makes us think about how ordinary we are—mere mortals who turn into ashes and dust. This should humble us to know our place and live with humility. However, most people think that humility is weakness and arrogance is powerful. The question that most people ask is, "What can I do in a world where everything is going wrong today?"

The focus is more on materialistic values than on human values. There are few people who say, "I can do something to make a difference in our world." This 'something' should not be just about giving a little money and thinking you have changed the world. Rather, it should be about giving yourself with humble involvement and commitment to be the change you want to see in the world and make a difference.

People give money after looking at a child's face on a brochure and then boast about it in their social circle, about how they are helping to change the world. Forget changing the world, they may not even be making a difference to the life of the child.

All most of us do is to give a little money, get a tax receipt and then just wait for updates by that NGO. This is like giving money to a child begging at one traffic light, who is forgotten by the time you reach the next traffic light. What about looking into the progress of the child and asking for accountability?

What about involvement with the child to ensure that the child eventually gets her place in the sun and is empowered to live a life of dignity? A small number of people do get committed to a child and look into the progress of the child with far greater interest, but most do not even try and visit the child even once.

Isn't such charity arrogant? It might make you feel

good and we may continue enjoying our materialistic life thinking we have done our bit, but have we?

We observe Earth Hour, click pictures in the darkness, then put them up on Facebook and claim that we have done our bit for saving the Earth and then every day of the year, we have all the lights on in all our rooms while we sit huddled in one room for dinner—do we give even a little thought about how saving electricity every day could have benefited others? Several businessmen are usurping other's natural resources, impoverishing communities and harming the environment with their bad business models.

They then do 'lip-service CSR' by feeding a couple of hundred children, even as they have displaced and harmed thousands of other children. Companies should ask themselves if this is not arrogant and faddish charity.

There are several things going wrong in our society and world today. It's now time to stop being indifferent and apathetic and change our mindset to understand that each of us has the power within us to right wrongs in our own space and time.

If all of us begin to right wrongs, then all together as one, we can right every wrong and that is when we shall truly enjoy the real feeling of the joy of giving. Let us include the need for doing good service to society in our purpose in life. Then you will notice how fulfilling your life becomes in every way. You will unleash the power and greatness within you and become extraordinary and limitless.

This will also help you find contentment, happiness and purpose in your life. Remember, you can't invent the purpose of life, but you can rediscover it while you do something meaningful by contributing to the greater good.

So, let's go beyond just giving or donating money to a charity or institution. Get involved. Be committed. You have the power to make a huge difference. Dream more, get inspired and inspire others also to be the change. Because, together as one, we can right every wrong by experiencing and spreading the real joy of giving.

Give With Love and Commitment

Oswald Pereira

Dear Bill Gates and Warren Buffett,

Each time you visit India and open a window to your fortune for philanthropic causes here, smiles light up the faces of those who might benefit from your generosity. Then as soon as you've gone, the joy you brought them goes, too. Why, despite the generosity of 'financial saints' like you, you end up leaving a large void in the lives of those you set out to uplift? Why are they not content? Are they not satisfied with your generous aid?

Mother Teresa figured it out in a way when she said, "There are many in the world who are dying for a piece of bread, but there are many more dying for a little love."

But then love, too, soon turns out hollow, unless sustained by something more substantial, like commitment. You have both committed a great deal of your wealth to help those in need of material help. Isn't your philanthropic legacy, the greatest act of love and commitment to date?

I'm not so sure.

For, to sustain love and commitment, one needs to share knowledge. And knowledge-sharing is not all about imparting education as we understand it to mean. Perhaps the answer lies in the *Bhagavad Gita*. In Chapter 4, Krishna talks about transcendental knowledge and says that material giving should be transcended by a higher form of giving.

Krishna tells Arjuna: "O chastiser of the enemy, the sacrifice performed in knowledge is better than the mere sacrifice of material possessions. After all, O son of Pritha, all sacrifices of work culminate in transcendental knowledge." (*Gita*-4:33)

The *Gita* makes material *yagya* or sacrifice the lowest form of giving. Vedic scriptures do talk of meritorious rewards one reaps with ritualistic sacrifices, rigorous asceticism or by philanthropic charity. However, the one perfected in the science of uniting individual consciousness with Ultimate Consciousness transcends them all and achieves the supreme, primordial abode *(Gita-8:28)*.

The *Gita* devotes an entire chapter to *Karma Yoga*, the path of action. As you mature on this path, you continue to perform good deeds—philanthropy may be one of them, but with less doership. Charity can be transformed to a spiritual plane only if it leads to reduction of one's ego and doership; doing good with perfection but without attachment.

The *Bible* puts charity on a high spiritual plane: "And though I have the gift of prophecy, and understand all mysteries, and all knowledge; and though I have all faith, so that I could remove mountains, and have not charity, I am nothing." *(1 Corinthians 13:2).*

However, in most versions of the *Bible*, the word charity is substituted with the word "love". It seems then that the *Bible* elevates charity to an act of love. The gospels favour silent giving, thereby delinking the act of giving with doership, as does the *Gita*. "When you give to the needy, do not let your left hand know what your right hand is doing," says the *Gospel of Matthew, 6:3*.

Said Satirist Thomas Carlyle on giving: "The work an unknown good man has done is like a vein of water flowing hidden underground, secretly making the ground green."

In Giving You Receive

Smita Jayakar

There once lived a wealthy man who was extremely stingy. He would never share anything with anyone. One day, he had a strong urge to eat *kheer*, but he did not want to share it with anyone.

So he gathered all the ingredients and went deep into a jungle to enjoy his *kheer* all by himself. The aroma of the delicacy wafted down to a sage who was sleeping nearby. Drawn by the aroma, the sage reached the spot where this man was cooking. He promised the man a mantra to secure unending wealth in exchange for some *kheer*. After weighing the pros and cons, the miser reluctantly convinced himself to share the *kheer*. The sage tasted it and exclaimed, "It's out of this world."

Overjoyed by this praise, the miser offered him some more. The more the sage enjoyed the *kheer*, the more pleasure the miser got in sharing it. He had never known this joy before. All thoughts of wealth were forgotten. That is the beauty of sharing. It benefits the giver more than the receiver. That is why charity is considered a virtue.

Charity is a form of *seva* or service to people. Giving money is not the only form of charity. Sharing food, giving knowledge, or even sharing a genuine smile is considered *seva*. One of the best forms of charity is imparting knowledge or helping someone find a job. As the proverb goes, "Give a man a fish and you feed him for a day. Teach him how to fish and you feed him for a lifetime."

Knowledge is neither wasted nor depleted. When you share knowledge it remains with the person for life. *Seva* should be provided in such a way that it benefits the person overall. Sometimes a person becomes dependent if you keep fulfilling his materialistic demands. Instead, one must do *seva* that makes a person's life meaningful and complete.

Invariably when we help someone, we expect at least a thank you. We feel hurt when we do not receive gratitude or appreciation. But charity has to be forgotten the very minute it is done. If you remind yourself and the world about how much you have helped, then the value of it is lost. People provide hefty donations to temples with the expectation of receiving *darshans* by preference. This is not charity but a form of bribery.

My Guru, Shri Dadashriji says any help given to

anyone with an ulterior motive is not considered charity. Our intention in doing charity matters most.

For some people charity may not come from the heart and there is nothing wrong in that. For such people I would suggest—start the practice with no intention and see how you will slowly draw pleasure from giving. Anything that gives you happiness becomes addictive and then giving will naturally become a part of you.

Give Silently

Reena Singh

A healer I know often tells me that for the very rich, to give away lakhs is not all that difficult. So she often asks them to do *seva* in a form that helps them learn a thing or two about themselves.

She charges them no money for her healings, but tells them to feed a cow or any other animal, but only after kneading the dough and making the *chapatis* themselves. They find this tough; for them, giving money away is the easy option. She charges the middle class, however, for she says they need to know the value of money in a different context—and to learn to let go. She passes on the money to charity, keeping just five per cent for herself.

It set me thinking. Isn't the opposite more true, that unless you have money yourself, there is not much you can or want to give away? On the other hand, shopping for several thousands in a single afternoon, taking a quick weekend holiday abroad, or replacing your phone for the latest gizmo on a whim is now possible even for the middle class, so giving away a few thousands in the name of charity should come easy too.

Yet, most of us are still reluctant to give things away and we find all kinds of justifications for it. Does the receiver deserve it, we ask ourselves. What does the gurdwara or temple *pujari* do with the money we put into the *hundi*? We are often riddled with suspicion and get visions of fat, corpulent temple priests spiriting away some of it at the very least. Remember the news reports of thousands of crores of rupees and the countless kilos of gold in temple vaults?

We see the misery on the face of the beggar on the road, yet we tell ourselves to ignore that plaintive cry for help and look sternly ahead, for he will merely use that money for his next fix. It might be true, but then again, it might not be.

October 2nd to 8th is officially India's Joy of Giving Week, now named *Daan Utsav* since 2014. The *Bhagavad Gita* talks of *tamasic*, *rajasic* and *sattvic* giving, so it may be in order to think of our own motives behind giving during the week. The Joy of Giving week was launched in 2009, but not many know about it. In 2013, the giving week netted just Rs 30 crores—a sum ridiculously low for our teeming lot of well-placed Indians, our ever-growing middle-class and our profit-heavy corporations.

Gandhiji's birthday ads are splashed across national dailies on Oct 2nd, but not a single ad is issued by any corporation or philanthropist to mark the start of the Joy of Giving Week. Perhaps, that is right. For giving should be done quietly, without fanfare and without much ado.

Do your own *seva* unobtrusively, either in terms of money or service. The moment you make announcements, earning yourself brownie points in a bid to enhance your status in society, it becomes an ego trip.

A giving event needn't be extravagant either, reason philanthropists. All it takes is a simple, spontaneous plan like taking your house help's children out for ice-cream or giving English lessons to your maid, once a week, to get started.

Maybe, we can eventually learn to keep the joy of giving week going, week after week, all year round.

It isn't a new idea, either. The United Kingdom has celebrated a National Giving Week, while Australia, Canada and a host of other countries have designated Giving Days.

In India, Jeroninio Almeida of iCongo thought of a Social Giving Day and campaigns like Karma Mitra and Joy of Giving to help raise donations for the needy and create awareness. Back in 2005, a handful of NGOs even got together to start a National Philanthropy Week with a few participating corporations. The idea finally turned into a nationwide India Giving Week in 2009, and, it seems, it is here to stay.

Give and Grow Rich

Reena Singh

All religions, ancient and modern, have remarkably similar views on tithing, which is the practice of giving away a tenth of your income to charity.

People—ordinary, everyday people all over the world—willingly open their hearts and their wallets to fill up the donation boxes at thousands of shrines, mosques, temples and churches, day after day.

A few of the world's richest people have gone a step further than that. They have pledged almost all their money to charity, leaving just a fraction for their heirs.

Philanthropists Bill and Melinda Gates now tour the world, more to oversee the charitable work of their Foundation than as representatives of Microsoft. Warren Buffet, the world's second richest man, has pledged 85 per cent of his fortune to charity. That's a lot of money to give away to charity! The Gates live modest lives. Buffet still lives in a five-bedroom house he has had since decades and drives himself to work. "I want to give my kids enough so that they feel that they can do anything, but not so much that they do nothing," Buffet says about leaving money to his heirs.

Closer home, four women have made it to the Forbes Most Philanthropic People in recent years—Kiran Nader, Rohini Nilekeni, Anu Aga, and Kiran Mazumdar-Shaw. The men include people like Sunil Mittal, Shiv Nadar, and Anil Agarwal.

Dashamamsha was the traditional Hindu practice of tithing, giving one-tenth of one's income to a religious institution. This spiritual practice, known as a *vrata*, was widespread in India.

Pull out the balance sheet of any big temple and you will see people giving generously and cheerfully. The abode of Lord Balaji, the Tirupati temple, is the richest Hindu temple trust in the world and manages a bounty of Rs 700 crore every year—all money that comes in as donations from devotees. This is apart from the jewellery, grain and other offerings that people gift to the temple. The temple owns jewellery worth Rs 50,000 crore in its vaults, including antique jewellery—again through offerings.

"People, especially the rich put handsome amounts of money in the *hundi*," says Subbarami Reddy, politician, altruist, industrialist and filmmaker, who has served as chairman of the Tirumala Tirupati Devasthanam and been a board member for years.

"Many of our rich businessmen are not used to charity work directly, but they do offer a lot of money as donation to the Tirupati Temple," he says. "God's money then goes to charity," he adds.

The temple trust runs several hospitals, and homes for the aged and the differently-abled. It also funds green projects. The *Old Testament* refers to tithing in the Books of *Leviticus, Numbers, Deuteronomy, Nehemia* and *Malachi*. But in the *New Testament*, Jesus Christ emphasises "Justice, mercy and faith, rather than mere tithes," says Father Shaji Antheenattu of the Catholic church.

Christ, in fact, was critical of the rich robbing the poor, and then easing their conscience by giving away a tenth of their wealth in tithes. Here, too, we hear stories of underworld dons attempting to atone for their sins by doling out a fraction of their loot to the poor. This, however, violates both the letter and spirit of tithing.

There is the *dasvandh* in Sikhism—besides their regular practice of *seva* and helping and contributing to the *langar* or community kitchen run by the *gurudwaras*—the *zakat* in Islam, and references to generous giving in almost every faith including Buddhism and Jainism.

New age beliefs such as Reiki and Pranic Healing have

their own versions of tithes, terming it as acts of loving kindness. "Pranic healing master Choa Kok Sui, for instance, would ask followers to donate at least 10 per cent of their income to the needy," says pranic healer Sangeeta Bansal, who is associated with the Manila-based World Pranic Healing Foundation.

"Master would recommend sowing in the name of God—the good karma then comes back to you multiplied many times," she says. "Consider donations as an investment. For all your rebirths to come, you will never sleep on an empty stomach," Bansal adds.

"Giving freely, generously, and cheerfully is the essence of tithes," reiterates Pastor Arvind Balaram of the Delhi Bible Fellowship. He advocates "Giving from your heart" and tells the members of his parish to choose any channel—the church, direct donations or through an NGO.

Bangalore-based Guru, Shri Nimishananda, says, "People think charity means donating money or clothes to the poor. This is charity, no doubt, but even if you've wiped a single tear or removed a little pain, you've made a difference."

And that's what tithing is all about. Begin with what you can donate—even one or two per cent of your income is a great start, but give with respect, love, gratitude, and feel honoured that you have been given a chance to serve your fellow men. It's not just money; you can give your time, knowledge, or simply teach. There is no greater joy in the world than seeing someone go for higher studies, or swing a better job with a bit of help from you.

While there are any number of miraculous stories posted on the Internet on the joy and rewards of giving, there are also detractors who say the poor should work hard to better their lot and not depend on others. A site dedicated to spread the joy of giving also lists some thirty excuses people quote for not giving or for postponing that decision by one more year.

The late Claude Rosenberg, a Stanford University business graduate and American philanthropist ran the New Tithing Group, an outfit that began persuading the rich that they could significantly increase their charitable work by giving while also shrinking their tax bill. Rosenberg was also the author of *Wealthy and Wise: How You And America Can Get The Most Out Of Your Giving.* The book details how wealthy people can afford to give more to charity through sound budgeting. Incidentally, their research showed that the middle income group gives away a bigger chunk of their savings than do wealthy people!

Most NGOs use this tax-saving concept—Save Money while changing a life—as a slogan to raise money. A website runs a payroll giving programme in leading Indian companies. Employee donations are channelled through their monthly salaries, making donations a regular habit.

Their philosophy is: "Everyday acts of kindness can turn into a wave of good."

Some employers send out mails that say: "Give away the cost of one movie ticket or half a pizza a month to the poor."

However, the spirit of giving entails giving not just tangible items but perhaps more importantly it implies the sharing of one's time and skills. For the giver grows richer by giving than by not giving.

KARMA

The Best Karma is Love

Oswald Pereira

Karma is among the most used, yet misused and misunderstood concepts today. Yes, it is said that as you sow, so shall you reap. More simply it means what goes around comes around. Put more explicitly, it can be said that your deeds, good or bad, will be repaid to you in kind.

All this boils down to the principle of cause and effect, which is what Karma basically is. This is quite a scientific, yet common sense concept. For isn't it commonsense that tells you that if you plant weeds in your garden, it won't yield flowers?

You don't even need to know the law or concept of Karma to understand this. Karma has been propagated as a tenet by various religions so that people do good and shun evil. But it was never meant to be used to preach punishment or divine retribution. When the faithful are bluntly offered a bad or a good deal in this life or the next life because of bad or good Karma, it smacks of both religious and spiritual immaturity.

Imagine standing before a child with a cane and a candy, and saying, "Be bad and you get this cane on your palms; be good and you receive this candy!"

That's not the way to teach goodness to a child. But this is how, it seems, Karma is often being taught to the faithful. It's no wonder then that many of us are turning Karma upside down. A lot of people today seem to be obsessed with Karma and are attributing much in life to it. It has become like a bogey and many want to jump on its bandwagon.

Karma is, otherwise, a good concept.

It's good to know that good begets good and evil will only invite more evil and sorrow. So far, so good. But when you start using or rather misusing the concept of Karma to explain too many things, it can become an obsession, like a fetish.

A lot of poor people suffer in this world because of suppression and oppression of fellow human beings. This has nothing to do with karma. Yet, many believe that the poverty and misery of poor people is caused by bad Karma. It may be not right to give alms to a beggar, but to scorn the beggar and attribute his plight to his own bad Karma shows a lack of compassion. An uncompassionate person doesn't reflect good Karma.

The poor are not poor because of their Karma, but because of an exploitative society, where the poor keep getting poorer and the rich, richer. Why are some women exploited so badly by men? Is it because of the bad Karma of women? Why are some lucky to be independent and free from exploitation by men? Is it because of their own good Karma?

This has nothing to do with Karma but it is because of the way society treats women. Yet when women, for instance, suffer domestic violence or sexual violence, it's not uncommon for some to attribute it to Karma.

Karma, of course, has its place. But we should be careful when talking about Karma, discussing it and analysing cause and effect.

Nishkama Karma—selfless or desire-less action—the key teaching of the *Bhagvad Gita*, reflects the basic concept or essence of Karma.

But the best Karma is love and its more sublime manifestation—unconditional love. When we love God more than we love ourselves and we love our neighbours as we would love God and our own selves, the law of Karma may be rendered redundant and obsolete.

Karma Can be Your Friend

Dr Kaity Cama

Understanding karma and using it in a positive manner is a powerful tool not only in our spiritual journey but in our mundane lives as well.

Karma is an ancient Sanskrit word meaning action or deed. Karma can be used effectively as a friend for our personal transformation and for understanding the spiritual journey of the soul if we so desire. To do this, we have to understand the karmic cycle and work with it, rather than against it.

Whilst the emphasis is most often laid on action or deed, it is always wise to remember that there is a powerful vibration caused by thought, not by the action alone. Let us take a closer look at what karma really is, with particular reference to individual karma; and then family and country karma will automatically be easier to understand.

If we look at any of our actions, we will find that we often repeat certain actions at various times, and refrain from certain other actions altogether. For example, if we have felt offended or hurt by someone else's words or actions, and if we have responded in similar ways to them, we have begun a karmic cycle which is non-positive.

We have alienated ourselves from that individual. If, on the other hand, we allow our personality and intellect to respond with kindness from our hearts, we have begun a karmic cycle which is very spiritually as well as this-worldly pleasant.

Any action performed by us leaves a memory within us. Sometimes, that is a conscious memory, sometimes it goes into our subconscious mind. When memories are thus stored involuntarily in our subconscious mind, we act almost reflexively in similar circumstances.

Even when we do not actually perform a non-positive action, but just think non-pleasant thoughts, the vibrations of the thoughts constitute karma. We are infinite choice makers, and we have the free will to choose any thought. By choosing the right thought we save ourselves having to go through unhappy circumstances in life. And when one lifetime goes by without our having learnt that we are meeting our own previous choices in situations of life, then there is a 'carry-over' into another lifetime where we are forced and compelled by circumstances to learn a much-needed lesson. It is so much easier to learn voluntarily rather than be forced to learn. And learn we must; the soul desires the personality to learn it easily. And the real you and the real me are the soul, not the personality.

Thought and action both are causes. Every cause has an effect, and if we begin to make connections between our thoughts and the ensuing circumstances of our life, we will truly find it a blessing, because that knowledge will help us refrain from choosing those thoughts and actions which bring us turmoil, ill health and conflicts.

All karmic debts have to be paid, and there is no escaping that fact. Some of us pay these debts and do not realize how we can use karma for our benefit. When things go wrong with us, we just say, "What can we do, this is karma", instead of saying, "Okay, I choose now to learn what NOT to do." Both thoughts are choices, the former being an unconsciously generated one, and the latter being a consciously chosen one.

Meditation and prayer help tremendously in transcending karma. The identical karmic results may show up from past choices, but we remain in a mode of detachment, simply observing them, because through meditation and prayer our awareness and consciousness expands and we also have the realization of the right choice of thoughts, words and actions.

For a *karmayogi*, transcending karma is imperative.

The *karmayogi* consciously uses memories instead of being a victim of memories and repeating mistakes.

Working with it as a friend transforms karma into a strength that grants us greater spiritual insights as well as success in our earthly life.

You Can Clear Your Karmic Account

Reena Singh

A man engaged in devotional service rids himself of both good and bad actions even in this life.

—*Bhagavad Gita, 2:50*

This is one bank balance that accompanies the *atman* in its seemingly endless journey of births and rebirths. It's the bank balance of your accumulated karmas of countless previous lifetimes—some good, others negative and painful.

If you are really lucky, your account will also have some portions of *akarma* or spiritual and non-binding karma that will finally liberate your soul from its endless journey. But it is negative karma that you should bother about, for this is the binding karma that decides your fate.

"Our *atman* comes back again and again with its bank balance of karmic factors," said Nalin Nirula, Reiki sensei, grandmaster and *Bhagavad Gita* expert. That, in short, is the essence of the overriding eastern belief in the reincarnation of the soul.

But with planned healing affirmations, we can restore our inner state to a level where we are free of irrational, negative and hurtful responses to ourselves, and to the people around us.

"Our life events then automatically make us progress in a natural way, freeing us from our karmic bindings now and in the future," added Nalin.

We can make our life "beautiful, joyous and fulfilling," and change our good and bad karma into *akarma*, attaining spiritual upliftment—all in this world.

Nalin's powerful Karmic Quotient or KQ training takes seekers towards peace, joy and harmony, as it teaches techniques to create a connection between their inner and outer universes, and to heal themselves and others with the divine light of spiritual energy.

Jyotsana Singh, a teacher who has done both the Reiki training and the powerful KQ training, said: "The training was life-changing." It liberated her from fear, the one negative emotion that controlled many of her actions and responses in this world.

"I am more in control and love the feeling of peace and calm that I have now," she added. She said that as a healer, she is now always conscious of being in the "right consciousness" and of doing good for others, more selflessly. She cited one instance: "As a teacher, I often invigilate. But now instead of watching out for negativity such as cheating, I send out healing to the students in the exam hall so that they do well."

There are others who also report miracle changes in their life after the KQ training. Amarjit Singh, a corporate consultant, who did the KQ training, said: "There is a lot of self-realisation now. I finally understand where I am and where I want to be." He is now infused with a sense of "positivity and well-being". Both his sons, in their 20s, are also Reiki healers and practise meditation and healing daily. "I feel more awareness of what is happening around me and feel more intuitive. I have also lost my false sense of ego," said Karanjit, his son. "Life goes on now—more happily—along with my materialistic ambitions!" he added.

That's really the way life should be, for we are born to live a life of peace, happiness and joy, building on a foundation of honesty, compassion and integrity. We weren't meant to battle strife, depression and anxiety, or live a life of vituperative, negative thoughts. Life is beautiful, if only we would look at it that way.

So now you have a choice: You can either continue living negatively or reach out to the positive energy that you can draw into yourself through your crown *chakra*.

As you transform yourself with karma-healing energy,

the very quality of your life could change. "This energy is spiritual and unlimited," assured Nalin.

Get ready then and set about overcoming existing patterns of your karmic credits.

You are Linked to Your Country's Karma

Reena Singh

Are we linked to what others do, or what the greater group that we are a part of, does? For example, does the nation have a collective destiny or karma on account of actions taken by the government or group of policymakers?

If this were true, it would also hold that an individual, though he is part of the collective consciousness that makes up a group, could 'jump out' of his collective karma through his own efforts.

Believers in the karma-of-nations theory point out that just as we differ from each other because of our deeds, so, too, the economic development of each nation is unique as it is shaped by collective action, good or bad.

When we vote in a government and its members fall far short of our expectations, we are inevitably part of their misdeeds, intentional or otherwise. This would hold true even if you are one of those who did not vote, for by not exercising your franchise, you helped bring in a government that failed to deliver.

Either way, karma catches up with you. Only if you let it, though. For, as individuals, every one of us has it in us to evolve spiritually and transcend the worst of collective karmas.

Once upon a time, countries like Iraq, Iran, and Afghanistan were the "Big Apples" of the Middle East—wealthy, prosperous, full of beautiful, happy people and smiling children.

Today, they are a shadow of their former selves. Are they suffering because of their past national karmas? And would their 'enemies' have to face karmic consequences for having decimated entire peoples and their heritage?

Perhaps we should accept the truth that we are responsible for our own status and that each nation is responsible for the condition in which it finds itself.

And so, karma indirectly means accountability. Every person, every government and every nation should be accountable for its deeds. There is no individual without his karma; and similarly, there is no nation or government without accountability.

Given the collective destiny that we are part of, can we remain detached, each an island, creating good karma? Buddha's bodhisattvas who've attained *nirvana* choose to be with seekers, encouraging them to grab the lowest rung of the ladder of enlightenment.

Perhaps we could be 'trainee bodhisattvas', steadfast on a path that might be at variance with the country's, and in this way, free ourselves of the country's collective karma.

Seven of his siblings succumbed to a collective karma and submitted to cruel Kansa's death blow. But not Krishna, the eighth child. Much later, his entire family died in unhappy circumstances, again, a karmic consequence, but Krishna remained unaffected until it was time for him to 'die', albeit from an arrow wound.

LIFE & LIVING

Neither Success nor Failure Lasts Forever

Oswald Pereira

In today's competitive world, what's the best path to success at the workplace? *Sakama karma* or self-centred action may seem to be practical for those aspiring to instantly beat the competition, but it may also end up to be a case of short-lived success.

Sakama karma may not be bad in itself and may even seem essential to succeed, but the true karmayogi transcends desire to reach the exalted state of *nishkama karma* or selfless action.

Then success is not a primary objective; yet it is more meaningful, sustainable and long-term because when you put service above self, the more you give, the more you receive.

There's nothing wrong in being successful but when success becomes an obsession or pathological attachment, danger creeps in, like a hidden demon waiting to strike.

The *Bhagavad Gita* says, "One who performs his duty without attachment, surrendering the results unto the Supreme, is unaffected by sinful action, just as the lotus is untouched by water."

These are beautiful words and the most sound advice on detachment to the modern-day professional.

Detachment doesn't mean you should not aspire to reach the top in your career. Your journey must be suffused with a sound proportion of detachment. Being detached in no way means you should not pursue success. The real meaning of detachment is to realise that nothing is permanent.

Success, too, is not permanent. Don't successful people face ups and downs in their careers? A professional who practices detachment will take failure in his stride and when faced with success, he will not make a song and dance about it.

When you climb the ladder of success, remember that if you go beyond the last step without looking, you may fall flat on your face. As children, when we played the Snakes and Ladders game, didn't we fall to the lowest level from the top when the snake was there waiting for us just when we thought we had won? Success is like that game. You may be on top at a point in time, but could reach rock bottom if you don't watch your step. If you have learnt the practice of detachment, the fall will not hit you hard and you'll recover your loss and regain your position at the top soon enough.

Pranic healer, Choa Kok Sui says, "Detachment means de-attachment. Life is a series of attachments and de-attachments, a series of holding and releasing, of connecting and disconnecting…because things change, and often, for the better."

Detachment is one of the supreme ideals of Jainism. Non-possession implied by non-attachment is among the *mahavratas*, the five great vows Jain monks observe. Buddhist texts mention detachment or non-attachment as *nekkhamma* or renunciation. It means giving up worldly pleasures and living a sacred life, free from lust, craving and desires. In Zen Buddhist philosophy, detachment is termed '*wu nian*'—literally meaning 'no-thought.'

Are all these wise teachings feasible to follow today? The answer lies in you. So why not try to follow them, if not in letter, then in spirit?

Detachment is a process rather than a single event. We need to work at loosening our hold on perceived achievements and possessions gradually until we finally come free of the situation of needless obsession and attachment.

Detachment cannot be achieved in a day; it is

not a one-time affair but a lifelong slow, steady and conscientious endeavour.

Try it, but do it slowly, bit by bit, one step at a time… till you reach that level of maturity when you can look at both success and failure with equanimity.

Don't be a Slave to Your Money

Maulana Wahiduddin Khan

Everyone knows how to earn money, but few know how to spend it. This is the most common experience in every society. A wise person is one who discovers this fact and plans his life by taking a lesson from it.

Money is a great booster for a person; at the same time, money may prove to be a source of disaster as well. Initially, money is a source of strength. It is its use that makes it good or bad for a human being. People earn money by applying their wisdom, but when it comes to the use of money, people can be remarkably stupid.

Recently, I was invited by a friend to visit his farmhouse which had been built beside an important road. It was fitted out with all kinds of comforts and luxuries. But practically, it was like a white elephant. I said to the owner that this had been a serious wastage of money and that if he had built a school on the site, it would have been a much better use of his money.

If you spend your money for some constructive purpose, that is very good, but if you spend it on ostentation, then it is bad. It requires great wisdom and hard labour to acquire money. It is very strange then that one chooses to be stupid when it comes to spending that hard-earned money.

If you spend money for the betterment of society, it will enhance your goodwill and you earn respect and good karma. But if you lavish money on your near and dear ones, you will only be providing them with easy money—and easy money is the worst of all things, in terms of the consequences it could bring to them. It is good to have money, but if money makes you arrogant, then it is worse than poison. If, on the other hand, money makes you modest, then it is a great source of your personality development.

If you make money your sole concern in life, it means that you are underutilising yourself. Money, of course, is a necessity, but its acquisition should not be your sole purpose in life.

There is a saying, 'In comparison do we understand'. If you compare money with learning, you can easily understand the difference between the two. Money is a risky form of capital, for you can lose it through an expected or unexpected event.

But learning is a permanent asset. If you have an insatiable nature, apply it to learning and not just to acquiring more money, which is a dubious investment.

I know of a person who was born into an ordinary family, but who, in his later years, came by a lot of money and became rich. One of his friends complained that before he became rich, he had been easily accessible to everyone, but now it was very difficult to meet him. The wealthy person replied: '*Mere upar daulat ki bijli giri hai.*' (The lightning of wealth has struck me.)

Externally, wealth seems to be a good thing, but internally, it is otherwise. Every wealthy person lives under great stress.

Once I happened to meet a businessman who took me to see his godown. Although this godown seemed to be a junkyard, there, a poor labourer was lying on the ground fast asleep.

Seeing the labourer, the businessman remarked, "I envy him, because although I have a luxurious bed, I've never had this kind of sleep."

It's good to make money your servant, but it's bad to let it become your master.

Relationships and Practical Spirituality

Dr Kaity Cama

Many people feel that spirituality means retiring from worldly affairs. Apart from the *rishis* and pundits whose chosen paths are living in isolation or in ashrams, spirituality is a very practical way of day-to-day living.

In fact, spirituality actually enhances your daily life in what the everyday person might call 'magical' ways. This may sound mystical or esoteric, but spirituality is really a very practical way of enhancing one's worldly living.

For example, consider everyday interactions and relationships. Everybody seeks an ideal, loving and harmonious relationship and ideal interactions with all people. And it is absolutely possible to have an ideal relationship with another person in this lifetime by putting practical everyday spirituality into action.

One of the major reasons of friction within any

relationships or interaction between people is the issue of 'control'. The "why can't you think the way I do? Why can't you be more like me?" is the underlying spark which triggers off arguments and disagreements.

Now if we can introduce a couple of spiritual tenets for ourselves before the disagreement reaches high intensities of emotions, the first thing that we will remember about practical spirituality is that we really don't need to control anyone's way of thinking.

In fact, we cannot, no matter how hard we try, ever control another adult's thinking. If we can surrender our need to defend our point of view, if we can just listen, actually listen to what is being said by the other person as well as to what is not being said by him/her, it would reveal a great deal to us. And as we understand the other person more, a greater insight is born within us.

There are no hard and fast rules about this in relationships. There are many factors that govern friction, but the bottom layer is always that of an issue of power, or in simpler words, self-importance.

If we can surrender a little of our self-importance, life would be much happier. That is also practical spirituality in everyday life—less self-importance.

Spirituality in everyday life is practical, and many of you have already experienced it and are continuing to experience it.

All human beings desire to be loved unconditionally, and whatever we desire from the world is what we first have to give to the world.

The language of unconditional love is also the language of spirituality.

Save Your Country From Corruption

Oswald Pereira & Reena Singh

When a rich and famous person is caught in a corruption case, we become oh-so-self-righteous and exhibit zero-tolerance levels. We are quick to condemn him for his corrupt act, but have we stopped to look in the mirror? Don't we do *chota-mota* dishonest things anyway—like flicking office stationery, giving a cop Rs 100 for *chai-paani* when we sail past a red light, and download music and books that have copyright issues?

We think nothing of photocopying a book or study notes if it suits us. Our list of petty transgressions can be pretty long.

The point is, no one's perfect. But everyone deserves the benefit of doubt and a fair trial in law courts prescribed by the prevailing judicial system. Does an icon's popular status or powerful position, make him more accountable?

Are we not all equal before the law? While the last may be true, it is also true that celebrities who are seen as role models shoulder a far greater responsibility than ordinary mortals.

Their every action and utterance is lapped up by their fans, especially the youth, and when their dark side is revealed in full public view, it can have devastating effects on public morale. And that's the trouble, according to Yogi Ashwini of Dhyan Foundation.

"The *Bhagavad Gita*," he says, "clearly states that a society functions on the footsteps of prominent people, the ideal *adarsh purusha*. This was especially true during *Satyuga*, an era of trustfulness, in which rulers were guided by gurus and were not tied to *maya* or personal gains, and when the betterment of society and evolution of the individual were prime goals."

Today, he says, '*adarsh purushas*' are "the film stars, politicians, administrators, sportspersons, and fake gurus," and their common denominator is their single-minded pursuit of wealth—any which way. Trouble begins when the common man with a meagre income wants to ape their lifestyle.

Then why do the rich and famous take to crime and corrupt practices to tote up their disposable income, at the risk of losing their name, fame and future? Don't they have enough and more?

"It's because they lack self-awareness of what they really want out of life," says Pulkit Sharma, a clinical psychologist. "They seemingly have everything, yet they experience an emptiness, a void. They feel they lack something. This feeling is at the core of their being and they think money will fill this void and bring to them freedom and happiness."

"Let he who is without sin cast the first stone," says Jesus to a mob ready to pelt stones at an adulterous woman *(Bible, John, 8.7)*. And so, let's ask that of ourselves each time we sit in judgement on our peers and celebrities for their transgressions.

For hasn't it been said that even a corpse will open its mouth when shown pieces of silver? How many of us can sincerely say that we have not indulged in corruption? When we buy or sell a house, do we pay or receive the full amount by cheque? Have we not paid speed money to get a quick water or electricity connection for our new, big *kothi*?

These are all corrupt acts and crimes punishable under the Indian Penal Code. Another favourite topic of discussion everywhere is politics. We have the power to elect the right candidate, but we seldom do research to back our choice. Often, we even abstain from voting, and then tie ourselves in knots when those in governance are caught with their hands in the till.

Also, corrupt politicians are corrupt because there are

bribe-givers. So, while gunning for politicans, jog your memory: Haven't you pulled strings too for a certain job or trampled a deserving candidate's CV so that your own son or niece can make it to the shortlist for a coveted interview or for a school or college admission list? These young ones might become the leaders of tomorrow.

The fact that the seed of their education was sown through a corrupt act is forgotten, because it's all part of the system, you know. That's what it is. Systemic corruption has come to be accepted as the norm. We go through our lives paying a price in many seemingly innocuous situations.

Yet, we consider ourselves squeaky clean! India is ranked low on the scale of honesty and probity in public and private life with 79th place in the Corruptions Perception Index for 2017, a global study of 168 countries by Transparency International. Foreign investors and multinational corporations find it hard to navigate the maze-like red tape here and so end up going to other, more business-friendly destinations.

The *Rig Veda* describes bribe-takers as thieves. The *Sama Veda* says it is a disease that goes on spreading, weakening both the soul and the human spirit. Both bribe givers and takers are tarred with the same brush. Is it because we are predisposed to corrupt practices?

So, the next time you promise your child the latest playstation—if he stands first in class—stop and think. You may be sowing the seed of corruption in a young, innocent and impressionable mind.

But don't lose hope, for there is a way out. "Instead of taking corruption head on to change the system, change at least one person around you and ask him to change another and so on…," says Yogi Ashwini. "But you have to change yourself first," he adds.

Sri Sri Ravi Shankar tells you to counter corruption with the five C's: Connectedness, Courage, Cosmology, Compassion and Commitment. "The first C is for a sense of connectedness. Corruption begins where a sense of belonging ends," he says, "and the last is for commitment to contribute to society," he adds.

That, together with a sense of responsibility for society, completes the picture. "You are going to inherit the country, so save it from corruption," urges the AOL founder.

How to Create Miracles in Our Daily Life

Dr Kaity Cama

All ideas, all thoughts, have their vibrations at their unique frequencies. A thought of anger has its own frequency, the properties of which are destructive for the individual, while a thought of peace or calm has its own beautiful frequency of vibration which is constructive and creative.

When we are being constructive and creative and doing things to the best of our ability, more spiritual knowledge and ideas begin to flow into us. Those who are just starting out, or have recently begun to start out on this path may find that they get ideas and thoughts which are not spiritual in nature. The reason for this is that we sometimes slip back into our old pattern of thinking.

The way to find out whether the idea or thought that has come to us is spiritual in nature or not, is by measuring that idea or thought against the spiritual ideal we have established. For example, let us take a real-life case. A young lady had a lot of trouble with her mother-in-law and sister-in-law, both of whom she said had 'ganged up' against her and would complain about her to her husband. This caused a lot of domestic friction between her and her husband. The husband would get stressed out, would not be able to relax, and gradually his work at his office began to drop in quality. The young lady in question was very depressed, very unhappy indeed, by the circumstances which had surrounded her in her married life, and it had reached a point where she was seriously considering a divorce.

She decided to give it one more chance for three months only, before actually approaching a lawyer for the divorce. She took up meditation on a daily basis even though she found it difficult in the beginning. At the same time, she established a spiritual ideal for herself. That ideal was harmony. Every morning, she woke up half an hour earlier for the meditation, and made a daily intention to think, speak and act in accordance with the qualities of harmony.

What are the characteristics of harmony? They are evenness of nature (not being temperamental or having outbursts of temper or tears), and a complete absence of discord in the mind.To achieve this, she realised that being of service to her husband, mother-in law and sister-in-law were of paramount importance, regardless of their behaviour towards her.

Her intention and desire to save her marriage was so strong, that within a week, her thoughts centred not on her happiness but on the happiness of the household. Instead of complaining about others to her husband, she became very supportive towards him. Instead of bursting into tears every time there was a taunting remark from her in-laws, she would think, "How can I serve them? How can I make them feel happier within themselves?" Remember this: it was not "How can I make them happier with me?" but "How can I make them happier and create harmony within themselves?"

Two weeks went by, and gradually the taunts became fewer and less hurtful. Towards the end of the month, an amazing incident took place. The husband realised that both his mother and sister were unnecessarily interfering in his marriage, and made a decision to move away to an apartment with his wife.

The mother and sister were worried. And the young lady said, "This is my mother, and my sister too. I will never leave them to fend for themselves alone in this house." The husband, his mother and sister were all astonished. From that moment on, everything just fell into place. It was not just the words that she spoke, it was the fact that she actually meant them as they were real vibrations of her thoughts.

This case had a happy ending and today if anyone, including her husband, dares to say anything to this lady, the mother-in-law and sister-in-law (who is now married and living away from them) defend her immediately. It happened once that dinner was a little late, and the husband made a comment jokingly about his wife delaying the cooking. The mother said, "Dinner is not late, it is you who have come home early!"

What did this young lady really do? She made a small shift of awareness, a small shift in her consciousness and this small shift led to greater awareness of spiritual ideas and thoughts. Putting herself in the background, she put the peace and harmony of the household in the forefront. That one single thought brought her more and more thoughts of similar vibrations. She actually raised her vibrations to such a level, that in her presence everybody felt calm and joyful.

Is that not a glorious way to live? And the young lady herself is so much more fulfilled, more at peace with herself and with all around her, contributing to the welfare of others. Her health has improved dramatically. There is more money coming into their home with all material comforts, and she has begun to teach meditation to both her young children, along with instructing them to uphold small spiritual ideals, which are possible for their ages. This lady is not a spiritual leader; she is an average wife and mother. And she changed her entire life simply by making one determined effort to save her marriage.

So you see, one does not need to be a guru or great

sanyasi to create what seems like miracles. These miracles are the natural forces of nature responding to our determined intentions when we wish to change our life for the better.

The vibrations of our spiritual ideals give form and substance to the ideas that proceed from it—it is a natural phenomena in our mundane life.

The Goal of Married Life

Maulana Wahiduddin Khan

Married life is not just about travelling together. It is about resolving issues and sharing of ideas.

It is true that adjustment is the only formula for a successful married life. But it is not adjustment for the sake of adjustment—it is for a higher purpose, that is, to create a normal environment in which it will be possible to achieve the real purpose of married life.

Married life is not simply co-travelling. It is rather co-sharing. Both partners in a marriage possess something unique and each needs to share that with the other. Each one of us is born with different qualities, and each one needs to share them with one's partner, so that both may develop their personalities in a better way.

One very important aspect of marriage is what I call intellectual partnership. Every day, we face problems; every day there are some new issues—we have to take some decisions, we want to explore some new area in the world of ideas.

This is important for both man and woman. Each one of us needs to have an intellectual partner with whom we can have a dialogue, and try to discover better options. And the best intellectual partner is none other than your spouse.

Everyone has adopted what may be called the adjustment culture—the businessman with his customers, every working man or woman with his or her boss. I think this is good, although the goal of this adjustment is only the money to be earned. But this adjustment culture is essential also between husband and wife. By adopting this adjustment culture in married life, you can earn something that is far more important than money.

When you converse with your partner, it is bound to give rise to new ideas. In this sense, the process of intellectual partnership leads to intellectual development. And, intellectual development is the greatest goal for every man and woman. Human beings are, by nature, explanation-seeking. So when you talk about adjustment in married life, both partners could ask, "Why adjustment?" You have to give a good explanation, otherwise any talk of adjustment will not have the right impact upon them. They may agree with your sermon on adjustment, but they will not follow it in their practical life.

My experience is in the field of scholarship. I know that study is the basis of scholarship, but only book-reading is not enough to develop a high level of scholarship. This requires exchange and dialogue. This is the concept of those activities which are called seminars and conferences. But your spouse is an ever-ready intellectual partner available day and night. Home-conferencing is far more beneficial than the formal conferencing which takes place in an auditorium. Discover this aspect of married life and any amount of adjustment will seem to be insignificant.

Life is a Divine Game

Amar Kumar

Football, cricket and other games have always had millions of fans. During the sports season, there is a lot of talk about the frenzy that grips most parts of the world.

The fiesta sees a whole range of emotions—from exuberance to pain, not just in the handful of men who play, but in millions of those who watch them. It is in this context that I wonder about the connection between spirituality and sports.

The image that games like cricket and football evoke is that of twenty-two sweaty, aggressive men, galloping around a vast field, chasing a tiny ball while thousands around them scream and hoot, clenching their fists and grinding their teeth. The roar of the audience echoes across millions of homes where eager faces sit glued to the television screen. It is a testosterone-fuelled, fiercely contested game where competition is severe and pressure is enormous.

It may be difficult to see the connection between sports and spirituality at first. But it exists. Ask the man whose attention is so completely focussed on hitting that ball into the net or out into the field. The world for him is distant, the ball looms large and everything else fades away. His body and mind come together. At the peak of tremendous physical effort, he focuses on one thing, and one only. Everything around him is immaterial. He finds his white light. As each muscle strains and pushes the boundaries, and as his blood pounds in his veins, there can be a moment of quiet, when silence descends and his foot or bat makes contact with the ball.

Sports can enable us to attain a higher state. Swami Vivekananda once said, "In kicking a ball or playing a game, you are much closer to the divine than you will ever be in prayer." You might mutter your prayers without being involved but there is no way you can score a goal like that. Not all of us are footballers though, but we can still incorporate a bit of it in our lives. We've all been told to 'be a sport', and for good reason. After all, being a sport means you are willing to play. Life is a game, with many twists and turns; we lose some and win some; it brings joy and pain. And just when we are exhausted, it asks: Do you want to play some more? Remember, in life's game, the ultimate goal is union with the divine and it requires *sadhana* with constant attention.

Spiritual Ego is Like Excess Baggage

Smita Jayakar

The most dangerous type of ego is spiritual ego. Every person on a spiritual path has to be very careful about developing it.

After many years of spiritual practice or reading many spiritual books, or sometimes even after reading one book, we start feeling that we are a level above everyone else. We generate an attitude of 'I know better' or 'What does he know!' That is why spirituality begins with awareness. We have to keep a very careful watch on ourselves about feeling greater than others.

When I first met my Guru Shri Dadashriji, after many years of being on the path, he told me: "Come to me only with a clean slate. Forget about your entire spiritual journey and what you have learnt, otherwise I have nothing to offer you. I am going to make you start from scratch." A person with spiritual ego holds on to his knowledge and will always make it a point to add his bit. I have experienced many such people in my workshops. They come with the intention to run me down with their spiritual *gyan*.

We once had a meeting with my Guru. He asked for a handful of us to come and meet him. We all felt extremely thrilled to be the selected few. As we all went in and settled down, the first thing he told us was to stop feeling so special. He said that the older you are into spirituality, the more baggage you have. He also said, "If you are close to him, it is only because you are unique cases and need more guidance."

This gave me the answer to my question which had bothered me for years as to why some big temples have money launderers as trustees. Why would God select such a terrible lot to be so close to him? It is only because they need help the most.

I've met so many spiritual people who do not share but exhibit their knowledge and experiences. They feel they have the answers to everything. Unfortunately, such people, under the pretext of spirituality, blind themselves from actual God realisation. They never accept another Guru's teachings. They block themselves out, thinking what they have learnt and what their Guru has taught them is the ultimate.

You have to realise there is no competition in

spirituality. With one-upmanship comes the struggle to prove superiority. It is very stressful to be on the edge all the time. Jealousy, insecurity, inferiority and other negative emotions are tagged along with a spiritual ego.

Many don't understand that there is always more to learn. If you are very knowledgeable, there's no harm in listening to what the other has to say and brush up on your information. Spirituality is a never-ending journey and you are always a learner. It should only make you humble.

Banish Your Ego, Build Your Self-Esteem

Oswald Pereira

One wise man said that there is a fine line between ego and self-esteem. Not true at all, for ego and self-esteem are on opposite sides of the fence.

A person with ego has a bloated sense of self-importance. But a person with self-esteem knows his true worth.

When you declare to your friend, "I am good," you are flaunting your ego. When you tell your friend, "We are good," it shows that you have so much of self-esteem that you grant the other person his goodness out of the largeness of your heart and soul.

Ego is destructive. Self-esteem is constructive.

A person with ego not only destroys himself—his core being, his inner, higher self—but also the people around him by trying to be one-up all the while, demanding attention and trying to prove his superiority by running others down, including his near and dear ones. A person with self-esteem has so much love and respect for himself that he can afford to share this with his fellow beings and be a channel of positive energy, spreading joy all around.

When we have ego, we don't respect another person's feelings or point of view, because we feel that would diminish our self-importance. The reason is quite simple: We don't have enough confidence in ourselves. When we have self-esteem, we are always mindful of the other person's feelings and are willing to consider his views, even if they seem at conflict with our own, because we are *gifted* with self-confidence.

Yes, *gifted*. We should consider, in all humility, self-confidence as a gift given to us by divinity, because we have become aware of our true, higher self that transcends our ego. The moment we consider self-confidence as an achievement, we tread on the negative, egoistic path that will send us on a downswing like the Sensex so often does.

In fact, ego is like the Sensex, highly susceptible to upswings and downswings. It makes our life uncertain and quite often it crashes, because it is a very unstable index of our happiness and well-being.

On the other hand, self-esteem is always so uplifting and will never let us down, as it is so stable, simply because it is based on our own self-worth and not what others think of us. Ego can be quite a spoiler—a spoiler of our peace of mind, a spoiler of our growth—emotional, psychological and spiritual. A person with ego shows signs of self-delusion, whereas a person with self-esteem has no illusions about himself—he/she knows and accepts himself/herself in an 'as is and where is condition', which paves the way for self-betterment.

It may perhaps be a good idea to start banishing our ego and building our self-esteem.

Namaste!

Jeroninio Almeida

Namaste! Namaste means the divinity in me salutes the divinity in you, the God in me respects the God in you, the human being in me respects the human being in you. I honour the light, love, beauty, truth and kindness in you because it is also in me. By sharing Namaste, we remove the distance between us, and share mutual respect with humility. We are the same and we are one.

This in a nutshell is the meaning of the word 'Namaste', a word that originated from India and teaches one a whole lot of human values. I begin all my training programmes (be it in companies, schools, B-schools or colleges) and public speeches with Namaste, trying to explain to people how by practicing the simple little things our traditional wisdom teaches us, we can become a better race and reclaim our nation's character and wisdom that we seem to be losing.

I get low energy response when I first start with Namaste, but as I explain how most of the wisdom originated from India and the East, energy levels rise and people get more interested in knowing about our traditional wisdom.

We have taken practices from the West like Reality Shows, cheerleaders, soap operas, talk shows, dance shows, consumerism, you name it. However, we have not taken their best practices like volunteerism or community service. In the west, seven-year-old kids sell lemonade to raise funds for their favourite cause. In India, kids are compelled to dance item numbers in reality shows by their parents. The West has taken all our best practices like Yoga, Ayurveda, Public Administration, Public Health, Urbanisation and made it better.

In places where people are still in touch with traditional values, you can see more humanity and humility. For example, in Thailand every Thai national, be it the King or the street vendor greets you with a low bow and says *Sawadeeka*.

Thailand is a classic case study of how the people face adverse occasions with responsibility, humility and humanity. They come to each other's aid in times of need without any discrimination or disparity. We saw this during the Tsunami in 2004 and the floods in 2011, which are case studies in Leadership Learning today. In Thailand, people always stand in queues and never jump lines.

In India, we have lost touch with traditional values and our original learning and wisdom that is benefiting the world today. Since we have lost touch with these values, most people think it is their birthright to jump queues and usurp other people's rights. We try to make money to ferry people across in times of floods as has been seen in Bihar, Bengal, Orissa, Uttarakhand and Assam. We siphon aid money as people and NGOs and are essentially becoming a race of fixers. If we want to improve as a race, we need to get back to our roots.

The simple little actions always make the big difference. If we focus on being less materialistic and concentrate more on human values, only then will India become better and we will have less of the social ills and evils that are happening in our society today.

Yoga: A Scientific Philosophy to Transform the World

Juliet Dsouza

Man searches. It is in his nature to seek that which gives joy, peace and happiness. Sometimes, he easily finds what he looks for and is content. Often, he does not know where to look; or what is it that he should look for.

He is on the right path, if he turns to earlier seekers whose wisdom and direction is outlined in philosophy.

Fascinating, profound, practical and popular is the path of Yoga. The system originated in India over 5,000 years ago as one of the six orthodox philosophical systems. To the common man, Yoga is synonymous with mystery, as the discipline was practised by a select few in the isolation of forests, caves and mountains. For generations, the knowledge was passed down orally as a well-guarded secret.

Individual interpretation led to various schools of thought and several texts, each advocating a particular yogic culture with the singular aim of spiritual fulfilment. Karma Yoga is based on selfless action and duty done in absolute purity. Bhakti Yoga is for those with strong emotions and an attitude of devotion. Jnana Yoga is the path of knowledge. Raja Yoga is for self-realisation through mind-control and meditation. Hatha Yoga offers basic preparatory practices, which address the physical and mental preparation essential for all Yoga aspirants.

The focus in Hatha Yoga is on cleansing the body as a means to achieve a pure mind. There are defined processes for this internal cleansing of the nasal cavities and the alimentary canal. This prepares the individual for the practice of psychosomatic body postures and yogic breathing. *Ha* represents the life force and *tha* represents the flow of mental energy. The practices are aimed at body-mind coordination and awareness through a balance achieved at the various levels of our existence. Consistent practice and a disciplined lifestyle lead to clear thinking, harmony, attitude change, increased immunity and a sense of well-being.

There are various body postures that have evolved. These are not mere physical exercises. They are practices that lead to the stillness and calm essential for meditation. Though there are different styles and methods, all Yoga practices relieve stress, develop strength and flexibility and lead to an efficient working of all body systems. Yoga has no bar with regard to age, sex, nationality or religion. The practices should, however, be chosen keeping in mind age and physical condition.

Yoga is not a competitive sport. Individual capacity and limits should never be strained. The end result should always be harmony in body and mind. Disharmony manifests in the form of disease. At the mental level, yogic breathing and relaxation techniques work wonders in stress management. A balanced attitude is developed and the individual can handle situations effectively.

Socially, man must adhere to moral and ethical disciplines. The great sage, Patanjali, who systematised Yoga as an eight-fold path, lists these as the first two essential steps, each with five distinct disciplines. The rules for social conduct are non-violence, truth, honesty, continence, and non-hoarding. For individuals, the rules are cleanliness, contentment, penance, study of scriptures and surrender.

Yoga was used by the early sages to meditate. This original spiritual purpose is often forgotten. Yet, inspite of the modern focus on physical culture, an individual develops the calm and direction important to his daily living. People the world over have accepted the power of this philosophical science which addresses the 'whole' man. Ascertained by observation and experiment, Yoga is an effective tool for health promotion and prevention of disease.

"Health", according to the World Health Organization, "is not a mere absence of disease. It is a state of well-being at the physical, mental, social and spiritual levels." Yoga is the only complete science known to address all these levels with tried and tested techniques.

Visions and goals for a better world sometimes remain concealed in fancy folders. Much time is spent in conferences and conclaves, discussing and formulating a blue-print for achieving the peace and joy man so longs for, day after day. But looking around, one wonders what is choking this universal search.

Very simply, it could be that the paths to these ideals are polluted with egocentric selfishness, greed and individualism. And unable to contain the ghastly effects of these base instincts, man finds himself in situations beyond his control. He desperately needs to break free from the bonds of corruption, greed, crime, drug abuse, human trafficking, war and many more modern evils. Distressing is the fact that advances in technology place weapons within easy reach.

The problems are indeed global and call for an effective global solution. And from the manner in which Yoga has become popular, it is evident that there is immense power in this scientific philosophy to transform the world.

PEACE, HAPPINESS & BLISS

Peace: A Universal Religion

Maulana Wahiduddin Khan

Peace is a product of a positive mental attitude, while violence is the result of negative thinking. Peace is the natural state of society; violence is an unnatural state. Peace is as much in accordance with nature's plan as violence is against it.

When peaceful conditions prevail in a society, all activities take place in their proper form. But if the atmosphere of peace is disturbed, the normal functioning of society is disrupted. This law applies to man, as well as to the entire universe.

According to the scheme of nature, peace is the only secret of smooth functioning in human society as well as in the rest of the universe. Peace, therefore, is such a basic requirement of man, that it is crucial to maintain it in all situations. Without peace, there can be neither development nor progress. No excuse whatsoever justifies the use of violence, in individual or national life. Regardless of how unfavourable circumstances might be, an environment of peace is indispensable.

We must maintain peace unilaterally, for nothing that we desire can be achieved without it. We need peace as all positive activities can take place only in an atmosphere of peace, with normal relations to be established between people. When peace prevails, constructive activities flourish and existing resources can be used for development or other creative activities. A positive bent of mind will prevail, which will help develop academic and intellectual advancement.

If we fail to establish peace, we must face destruction in every field of life. The option for us is not between peace and no peace, but between peace and annihilation. Without peace, there is no hope for the survival of mankind. What disturbs the peaceful plan of nature is mainly traceable to the fact that people have become excessively materialistic. It is this thinking that leads to the exploitation of nature. If people opted for a path of moderation, they would soon discover that, if earlier they were comfortable physically, now they are comfortable spiritually. And without doubt, spiritual comfort is far better than material comfort.

The perpetrator of violence invariably suffers from remorse, while the peacemaker derives great satisfaction from his efforts. If one were to think of the end result, one would never indulge in violence. One should bear in mind that peace is in consonance with humanity, whereas violence means a descent to the animal level. Peaceful minds make for a peaceful world. A peaceful society is a result of peaceful persons. Therefore, peace can be established only when every single unit of society is ready to live in peace.

Only those persons can live in peace who are ready to remain patient regardless of the circumstances. The fact is that everyone is born with different tendencies and everyone is free to follow their preferences. That is the law of nature, due to which it is impossible to establish uniformity in society.

In such a situation, the question arises as to how peace is to be established in society? The only answer is the magic word: *sabr* (patience). *Sabr* is the key to having a peaceful society. A peaceful society requires avoidance of friction, tolerance, positive thinking, and the ability to retain one's emotional equilibrium, even when provoked.

Peace is the only religion for both man and the universe. In a peaceful environment, all good things are possible, whereas in the absence of peace, we cannot achieve anything of a positive nature, either as individuals, or as a community, or even at a national or international level.

We Are Our Own Source of Peace and Happiness

Oswald Pereira

What has peace got to do with happiness? The connection is like that between life and living. For, peace makes life worth living, and paves the way to happiness. Peace and happiness are linked so inextricably that there's no happiness without peace.

What comes first: peace or happiness? Could you be at peace if you're not happy? The answer to these questions depends on your idea of happiness—on whether you get happiness from external factors or from within.

In the *Bhagavad Gita*, Krishna tells Arjuna that no man can know happiness without peace. But, to experience peace, we need to prepare ourselves to receive it; so in a way we are responsible for making peace and happiness happen. For peace and happiness to last, both ought to spring from within, regardless of any turmoil or otherwise that is happening outside.

The more you internalise your feelings of peace and happiness, the more the chances are of your reaching blissful heights. Once you are able to source peace and happiness from within, you can transcend external vicissitudes to remain ever-happy and blissful.

Reverend Ernest A Fitzgerald described happiness as a 'deep sense of inner peace' that comes when you believe that you are 'making a difference for good in the world'. Thomas Jefferson, former US president, said that, "it is neither wealth nor splendour, but tranquillity and occupation that give happiness."

From a Buddhist perspective, too, one can learn that people inflict pain on others in the selfish pursuit of their happiness or satisfaction. "Yet, true happiness comes from a sense of peace and contentment, which in turn must be achieved through the cultivation of altruism, of love and compassion, and elimination of ignorance, selfishness, and greed", in the words of the Dalai Lama. The Buddha said that to "enjoy good health, to bring true happiness to one's family, to bring peace to all, one must first discipline and control one's own mind."

Peace is a recurring prayer in the Holy Mass celebrated by Christians. The priest chants, "Peace be with you" and the congregation replies, "With you also". The congregation offers each other 'The Sign of Peace'. The mass ends with a blessing by the priest, "Go in peace, the mass is ended".

What, then, happens to the non-believer? Is he doomed to unhappiness? It would be uncharitable to draw such a conclusion. For, there's peace in the smile of a child; there's peace in the tender touch of one's mother; and it's got nothing to do with God or religion.

Thich Nhat Hanh, the Vietnamese Buddhist monk says that, "If in our daily life we can smile, if we can be peaceful and happy, not only we, but everyone will profit from it. This is the most basic kind of peace work." Again, no religious strings attached to peace.

The Vedic idea of peace includes peace in all areas of life—psychological, social and environmental. The *Yajur Veda* declares: "Let there be peace in heaven, Let there be peace in the atmosphere, Let there be Peace on Earth... May the waters and medical herbs bring peace, May the trees give peace to all beings, May all the gods be peaceful, May the *Vedas* spread peace everywhere, May all other objects everywhere give us peace, And may that peace come to us and remain with us, forever."

Peace and Non-Violence go Hand-in-Hand

Rabbi Ezekiel Isaac Malekar

Peace and non-violence walk on the same pathway of goodness, like brothers-in-arms. But the arms here is not armament or weaponry, but, indeed, human arms that symbolise love. Peace is built on the foundation of non-violence.

Expressed the other way round, it is the belief and practice of non-violence that grows peace.

Peace and non-violence first need to be internalised, before they are expressed in positive action in the world. For us all to achieve the ideal state of non-violence and peaceful existence, we need to first start the practice in our mind itself, everyday, and at all times during the day.

The commonest Hebrew word in this context is '*Shalom*', which connotes peace in all its ramifications. *Shalom* means not only freedom from all disasters, but health, welfare, security and tranquillity. It is to be safe, sound, perfect and complete. Shalom signifies a sense of well-being and harmony within and without—in effect, holistic health of our body, mind and spirit.

The philanthropist, Moses Montefiore aptly described peace, as which 'alone reconciles and strengthens, calms us and clears our vision and frees us from the bondage of unsatisfied desire.'

The vision of non-violence and universal peace is well-expressed in chapter two of the *Book of Isaiah*. The prophet says: "...and they shall beat their swords into ploughshares, and their spears into pruning hooks: nation shall not lift up sword against nation, neither shall they learn war anymore."

The concept of non-violence is rooted in the commandments, "Thou shall not kill" and "Thou shall not covet." The prophet emphasised that the best way to destroy destructive ideas and inclinations is to replace them by peaceful, constructive behaviour.

The best non-violent way to respond to rudeness and violent action is to give a soft answer. "A gentle answer turns away wrath; but a harsh word stirs up anger." *(Proverbs 15:1)*

It is not enough to be merely passively non-violent. We must aim to make friends of our enemies and of those who wish to harm us. Rabbi Joshua said, "The evil eye, the evil inclination and hatred of his fellow creatures drive a man out of the world."

Mahatma Gandhi said that what is attained through violence and hatred does not last long but what is gained through love and peace is retained forever.

Rabbi Morris Joseph said: "Peace is one of the pillars of the world; without it, the social order could not exist. Therefore, let a man do his utmost to promote it. Thus it is that the greatest sages made a point of being the first to salute passers-by in the street."

Let us all pray to the Supreme Being that abundant peace descend from heaven. May God in his tender love create peace for all people of the world.

Spiritual Ideals Spark Happiness

Dr Kaity Cama

Spiritual ideals when held staunchly upright and constant in our minds and hearts, help us change our health, our circumstances and our happiness in daily life.

The *application* of such ideals in our daily activities is necessary, for it is that which brings about a change for the better.

Those of us who are not accustomed to establishing and holding very high spiritual ideals may find it difficult to do so, and may even give up within a few days' attempt. In such cases, it is better to start with smaller spiritual ideals. If, say, harmony is too high a spiritual ideal to maintain, then a much smaller one may be taken for starters.

For example, gentle thoughts and gentle words. In incidents where one's anger and indignation are aroused from the old thinking pattern, then instead of speaking out the anger, one should try to be silent at that moment, even if it's difficult. That is a big thing to do—it's one step towards upholding to a small extent the spiritual ideal of gentle words.

One of the greatest rewards that takes place is that we begin to draw to us ideas which help us to uphold our spiritual ideals. Spiritual ideals can and should be changed once the original ideal has become part and parcel of one's nature. One may then move to a higher spiritual ideal. Our education system does not provide such information to the young students, and children always think and act according to their parents' ways of being. Hence, parents ought to set a good example for their children, as this will help youngsters grow up into mature, spiritual persons.

And as we walk along this path, the ideas that keep flowing into us are not just for spiritual purposes—they are spiritual in nature, but they are of great utility in managing our daily living, in our relationships, in our health, in our money. Without spiritual ideals, we encounter obstacles of all sorts—physical, mental, emotional. As spiritual beings, we are meant to experience and enjoy material life. We can do that smoothly, evenly, easily, by holding spiritual ideals as our constant companions. As true spiritual knowledge and insight flows into us, our connection with our own divinity becomes so obvious and open to us.

As our own individual frequency of vibration changes

to higher frequencies, we become one of the "luckier, happier, more fulfilled" people, who seem to get everything they desire. If you study such people, you will find that their thoughts are very far from the zone of any negativity.

All negative thoughts arise when we, in human form, are vibrating at low frequencies. Whether it be our family environment, our social environment or the indoctrination brought about by films, novels, and society, and not consciously our individual choice, we can begin to use our conscious choice to feel, sense and recognise our true essence—that magnificence of omnipotence, without any limitations.

If we use the option of our free will to consciously be aware of the choices we are making each moment of the day, and make such choices which benefit not just our self, but benefit others too, we will be well on our way to creating a paradise on earth.

Granted that we cannot change others through advice or even through force. But each individual change to a higher frequency helps clear and clean the ether as well as contributing to group energy of family, community and country.

We are all constantly vibrating, and that is a fact. An added bonus is that when we are constantly vibrating at very high frequencies, earthly laws do not affect us.

By earthly laws is meant laws of gravity, visibility, and

so on. We are able to live in both the physical and the non-physical worlds simultaneously, in harmony with nature, the universal principles, and divinity, thereby fulfilling our true destiny.

Way to Happiness

Oswald Pereira

L Ron Hubbard, the founder of Scientology, observed that as the world lacked any moral guide to ensure survival and happiness, man was prone to a joyless existence.

This prompted him to write *The Way to Happiness*, a common-sense guide to happier living. Hubbard came out with 21 moral precepts of the way to happiness that were not tied to any particular religion. The 21 precepts may be likened to the edges of a road. "Violating them, one is like the motorist who plunges onto the verge—the result can be wreckage of the moment, the relationship, a life," said Hubbard.

But it was left to each individual to draw his own road map to make his life smooth and successful. What is different about *The Way to Happiness* is that it not only presents the precepts by which one may live a better life, it also explains why and demonstrates the very real correlation between virtue and joy. The precepts and their benefits are described in an everyday life context.

For instance, life is more enjoyable when you are physically healthy enough to participate in it. Harmful habits like taking drugs will only harm your health and thus your capacity to enjoy life and be happy. Likewise promiscuity goes against happiness, because it shatters relationships and families.

The easing of workplace tensions, religious and racial tolerance contribute towards a more productive and harmonious civilisation. The central theme of *The Way to Happiness* is solely a common-sense appeal to everyone to respect one another and help each other find happiness.

As Hubbard writes in the introduction: "It is in your power to point the way to a less dangerous and happier life. While no one can guarantee that anyone else can be happy, their chances of survival and happiness can be improved. And with theirs, yours will be."

The 21 Precepts of *The Way to Happiness*

1. *Take care of yourself*
2. *Be temperate*
3. *Don't be promiscuous*
4. *Love and help children*
5. *Honour and help your parents*
6. *Set a good example*

7. *Seek to live with the truth*
8. *Do not murder*
9. *Don't do anything illegal*
10. *Support a government designed and run for all the people*
11. *Do not harm a person of good will*
12. *Safeguard and improve your environment*
13. *Do not steal*
14. *Be worthy of trust*
15. *Fulfil your obligations*
16. *Be industrious*
17. *Be competent*
18. *Respect the religious beliefs of others*
19. *Try not to do things to others that you would not like them to do to you*
20. *Try to treat others as you would want them to treat you*
21. *Flourish and prosper*

My Quest for Happiness

Reena Singh

Happiness, happiness, the greatest gift that I possess
I thank the Lord I've been blessed
With more than my share of happiness
To me this world is a wonderful place
And I'm the luckiest human in the whole human race
I've got no silver and I've got no gold
But I've got happiness in my soul

Back in school in the '70s, a guitar-strumming young priest taught us this song, at a leadership retreat attended by a class full of starry-eyed 16-year-olds. Then came college, followed in quick succession by work, marriage, children and responsibilities—and my notions of happiness collapsed systematically like a house of cards. My favourite happiness song now sounded false and artificial. I found nothing lilting or uplifting in it anymore.

Is there a formula for happiness? Such as think positively. Keep the smile plastered on your face! Be nice to all and they will be nice to you! As you move from year to year and from crisis to crisis, you realise happiness exists, but finding it is not that simple. Happiness isn't something they sell in shops. You realise that while roses bloom in gardens, and even as you sit watching them, they don't really bloom within your soul.

You might begin blaming it all on yourself —why does it happen to me? Everyone else appears to be enjoying life. They are holidaying abroad, earning several lakhs in salaries every month, live at an enviable address, have children studying in the best of colleges, and so on and so forth. At this point, you can either hit the bottle, visit shrinks and reach out for your pills or wallow in self-pity and hit rock-bottom. Or you can take stock of your life. This is almost usually followed by a phase when you are looking for answers, scouting around for a happiness formula. Will more money do the trick? Will foreign holidays add zing to your life?

You now hark back to the old days. You realise you were born happy, but then you systematically foiled it up with your own foibles and follies. So, now, fulltime, you embark on a quest to find happiness.

But will you ever find it? It never matches up to your expectations, nah!

If you have money, your relations with your spouse or children are not up to the mark. If everything else may be seemingly fine, children might not do well in school and college, or you might end up with a health problem. It could be worse, but the practical among us will not fall prey to misery.

You brace up to fight the challenge. You turn to philosophy. You learn to be detached, to see the bigger picture, connect with nature and eventually find some semblance of happiness this way.

The message is simple: Don't give up, for tomorrow is another day—and eventually, the sun does shine again.

And even if the rain soaks the sun in dark showers, flashes of lightning will light up the sky for a while.

Then at night, the moon will glow in the sky and the stars will shine so bright... for, after all, there is always a happy ending to every story.

Bliss Vs Happiness

Dr Kaity Cama

The difference between happiness and bliss is, in very simple terms, that happiness is a feeling of the individual's personality, and bliss is the state of the underlying spirit. Let us then take a closer look at both happiness and bliss.

The individual's personality is woven around beliefs that are promoted by the ego. Most people equate their happiness with circumstances and incidents of their daily life—with how much money is in their bank, how many possessions they have accumulated, projecting a self-image which wins them applause and compliments from other people. Happiness is measured by success in our jobs and careers.

"If only you would think the way I do, I'd be happy."

"There's so much going on in the world! If only the world could be more peaceful, I'd be happy."

These and similar "if only" thoughts stem from invalid beliefs. A belief is just a thought that one repeats to one's self over and over again, or which has been deeply steeped into us from childhood by our elders, who perhaps themselves had these beliefs ingrained within them in their childhood.

Such beliefs cause us untold hurt feelings when the world does not respond to us the way we want, when our good-intentioned words are misunderstood by others and when we misunderstand others and build up walls around us. For most of the world's population, happiness depends entirely upon outer circumstances and other people.

When someone speaks rudely with us we feel either offended or hurt. The memory of that prevents us from finding happiness, and the more we dwell upon such incidents, the more we attract them into our lives.

When we seek external references for happiness, we lay ourselves wide open to disappointments. The applause and admiration we have when we are corporate leaders, have large bank balances and some worldly power, all disappear when we do not have them. Is it really, really worthwhile seeking the approval of others?

It may be argued that we live in society, and should be 'fitting in' with it. Society is man-made, however, and it takes just one per cent of society's population to set a different trend—be it a positive or non-positive one. A positive trend will automatically result in positive changes and results, enriching the individual's life.

Bliss is that zone where the individual sees the entire universe as a glorious experience. Bliss is simultaneously joy and serenity, which are attributes of the spirit. Even the smallest of glimpses of this zone changes the perspective of the individual, and we are all capable of reaching the zone whilst still in our physical bodies, leading our everyday lives.

We are, in essence, spiritual beings—beings of that Infinite Light of Intelligence which runs through our physical bodies and without which our bodies would decompose. It is that same Infinite Light of Intelligence, which runs through every being, through the entire universe.

This zone of bliss cannot be reached through the intellect unless one has aligned ego to spirit. It is far removed from the zone of happiness and in between these two zones is another zone—that of joy. Those of us who live our daily lives through spiritual precepts find ourselves bubbling with joy. Those of us who have embarked on this journey very recently will find that there are moments of joy alternating with their old patterns of thought; and those of us who have always lived life according to spiritual precepts will find that there is almost constant joy in everything.

Joy is the state of consciousness, which may or may not rationalise events and circumstances, but even in that rationalisation, there is overwhelming understanding, compassion and kindness towards all creation. This is the zone from where manifestation of one's desires takes place, because one's intention is actually in alignment with universal intent. Intention is a powerful force in nature, and author and scientist Rupert Sheldrake's experiments have proved it so.

When our intention is with the flow of the universe, our desires are fulfilled from the unmanifest into the world of so-called matter. This zone, once experienced, changes the individual's perspective completely, and paves the way for a higher state of consciousness—the zone of bliss.

These changes in consciousness can occur overnight depending on the individual. When one is in the zone of joy, one actually works in both worlds simultaneously. Everyday life is enhanced in every way. Raising our consciousness to higher frequencies is putting spirituality into action. Knowing about spirituality is good, and putting that knowledge into action is excellent.

A Moment of Bliss

Oswald Pereira

Many of us may spend a lifetime in pursuit of happiness. But it is just one moment of bliss that may be more fulfilling than a million hours of happiness. However, no amount of wishes and even endless hours of prayer to the Supreme Being can really bring in bliss.

There's no bliss in happiness. You may be the world's happiest person but that will not assure you even a split second of bliss... because there is absolutely no connection between happiness and bliss.

It is said that bliss begins where the expectations of happiness end. Seems so very true. However, this appears like building a boundary wall between happiness and bliss. But bliss has no boundaries and no walls.

Many believe that the pinnacle of happiness is bliss. Others surmise that bliss is a state of complete, perfect happiness. And some imagine that just like you climb the ladder of success after accomplishing great things in life, so also bliss is like a trajectory that is propelled by big bouts of happiness.

The touch and embrace of a loved one has often been described as a blissful experience. Parents find bliss in the smile of their child. There's no harm in imagining bliss in all manner of happy situations. But bliss is something that you can't imagine or even experience, because when it visits you, the five senses, and the mind and intellect are on a holiday.

You don't feel, touch, sense or experience bliss. It doesn't turn you on or move you to tears of joy. It is not within you, it is not outside you. It doesn't exist in the worldly sense of the term. It comes when you cease to exist; when you are beyond time and space; when you are detached from happiness and indifferent to sadness; when you realise that nothing matters—only God does.

And if you don't believe in God, then even God doesn't matter. For, isn't God an attachment that we cling to in the hope of attaining that one moment of bliss?

And when bliss knocks at your door, you may not even know, because if you do, then it is not bliss, but an illusion, your imagination growing wild.

Oh God, please bless me with that moment of bliss! Our prayer may only amuse God and drive bliss away. Just like it is easier for a camel to go through the eye of a needle than for a rich man to enter the Kingdom of God, bliss is not something that comes easy or a boon that God grants when you pray to Him.

Though we were born crying, we were closer to bliss then. For, bliss is the natural state of being. Let us stop chasing or imagining bliss. One never knows when God or nature may bless us with a moment of bliss. Bliss can be real if God or nature wills it. A wise person said that bliss is to be deeply at peace with the world and life.

There's bliss in all of us, but it lies submerged because of our ego and worldly quests and pastimes.

Bliss is attained "when the mind, absolutely restrained by the practice of concentration, attains quietude, and when seeing the Self by the self, one is satisfied in his own Self," says the *Bhagavad Gita (Chapter 6, 20-23).*

POSITIVISM

The Positive Side of Negative Experiences

Maulana Wahiduddin Khan

Thomas Alva Edison was among the most prolific American inventors of all time. With his inventions, Edison exerted a tremendous influence on modern life. More than a thousand patents are registered under his name.

But the early history of Edison presents a very different picture. After a few months of schooling, his teacher declared him 'addled' and claimed that he wouldn't be able to continue with his education in school. Edison's mother had no option but to take him out of school. She then decided to teach her son at home. This proved to be a great moment in Edison's life—while the door of one school was closed to him, at the same time, the doors of two other schools opened up—home-school and mind-school. As a result, Edison's mind was triggered further and he became motivated to learn on his own.

This incident presents an example of that miraculous factor in human beings, known as nature. The principle we derive from here is that when someone denies giving you something, nature comes into play to compensate for your loss on a far greater scale. According to the law of nature, there is always a positive aspect of every negative experience. The only condition is that one should not become negative or succumb to despair. Life is full of unpleasant experiences. There is no escaping them. But negative experiences are not evil phenomena. They are, in fact, a kind of blessing, a sort of intellectual challenge. In such situations, it is better to wait rather than opt for a reactive approach.

If you save yourself from becoming the victim of a negative experience and opt to do just one thing—that is, do nothing—and let nature take its own course, it will serve as a positive factor for your mind. It will certainly increase your thinking capacity and unfold your intellectual treasures. If you have developed a strong personality and an intellectually awakened mind, then every shock will prove to be positive for you and you will automatically absorb the shock as a new opportunity. This is because the law of nature stands above all else and when you choose to remain unaffected by an unpleasant experience, you invite the law of nature to come to your rescue and initiate a process to compensate for your loss.

Life is full of opportunities. Even if someone takes away

something that had been given to you by someone, what nature gives you can never be taken away. For example, if a person gave you a man-made torch and this is taken away, no one can take away from you that divine torch, the sun. Knowing this principle brings a feeling of immense hope.

The only fit response when you find yourself in a negative situation with others is to forget the unpleasant external experience, and on your own take a fresh decision to improve your abilities. Very soon, you will find that you have gained more than what you had lost.

There is no full stop in life, only commas. No event is the final chapter of your life's book, for every day, you are in a position to add a new chapter to it. This is due to the enormous capacity of the human mind. Don't underestimate your mind. It is when you underestimate your mind that life leads you towards frustration.

If you discover the capacity of your own mind, it would give you great courage and unending strength. You will be able to take a new leap into your future from the very point where you thought your life's journey had come to an end.

Positivism is to Say Yes to all Good Things

Dr Kaity Cama

Positive mental attitude is the foundation of all success, both spiritual and mundane. Research has shown that people who have a positive mental attitude have stronger immune systems, are more calm in the face of crisis, are able to make decisions of a high calibre, and have happier relationships in addition to being successful in their business and career.

When we have a positive mental attitude, we are saying *Yes* to all the good things in life. It is then easier to be self-disciplined, giving ourselves the advantage of going in the direction that is right for reaching our goals.

Those of us who have not yet had a taste of positivism, find ourselves filled with anxiety, anger, resentment and even despair. Those of us who have once had a taste of positivism never want to lose it, because it brings with it tremendous peace of mind. We find that peak achievers in life have as their constant companion the presence of positivism. They look exactly as other people do, leading normal lives, but they seem luckier, happier and more successful. Where others struggle, peak achievers just seem to sail through smoothly. What is the secret behind this?

Those of us who live with positivism do not waste time in proclaiming to the world what they can do. They just go ahead and do it, without waiting or asking for applause.

How can we cultivate positivism within our personality? The first step for us is to desire it sincerely. This desire makes us willing to make the effort. And it is not a big impossible-to-achieve effort either. When there is a real, heartfelt desire for positivism, that desire itself brings us the various opportunities that propel us towards it.

The opportunity may come through reading a book on positive thinking, it may come through reading an advertisement for a lecture or seminar, it may come through reading a poem or a biography of an inspirational character. Whatever form the opportunity comes in, it creates a shift within our consciousness, and that shift, no matter how small it be initially, begins to fill us with the wonder of positivism. As we see the results of that small shift in our daily life, we are filled with an increasing enthusiasm for more of the same.

Sometimes it happens that instead of a gradual increase, the shift in consciousness is total, and though it may seem overwhelming in the beginning as most quantum leaps tend to be for the average individual, we get very comfortable with it, though the wonder and the gratitude always remain with us. Gratitude for all the blessings we have received and continue to receive, brings more blessings in turn, linking positivism with the Law of Attraction, Karma, and Bliss.

The outstanding quality of positivism is that it brings us success at every step, in every field of endeavour, be it on a spiritual journey or on a worldly one. Positivism is part and parcel, as it were, of spirituality. Positivism implies turning away from darkness into the beautiful light of purity of thought, word and deed.

Being positive in our thoughts means looking at the beauty of life, expecting the best to come to us, and never wavering in our faith. When we replace doubt with a knowingness about the good, anxiety disappears, anger dissolves; there is that in our energy field which makes us feel calm and safe and happy.

A positive mental attitude boosts our self-confidence, making us more and more aware of our infinite abilities, our hidden talents and gives us the initiative to awaken them for our own and others' benefit.

A positive mental attitude takes all factors into consideration, and works out a solution. Positivism always finds solutions, and these solutions are always spiritual in their attributes.

Without positivism, we would be drifting along, sometimes this way, sometimes that way. To go anywhere worthwhile, positivism is the first cornerstone of a solid foundation for success.

Smile a Thousand Times Every Day

Yogi Dr Amrit Raj

A smile is the most beautiful, precious gift given to us by God and by nature. We can reach anyone's heart with a smile. Not only that, we can change our life and that of others, too, with just a smile.

When someone is depressed, fearful, or stressed out, all so common in today's fast-paced world, one must find the reason for the depression, then work towards removing the cause. Once this is done, depression will gradually disappear. We need to consciously look for reasons to smile.

People are always complaining and find no reasons to smile. They say 'Life won't change and this is how I am.' Don't keep saying you are unlucky. If thinking like this is programmed in your mindset, work towards changing it. If you think about it, you will find instances where you have been lucky too.

So, learn to be positive. Follow this by being very positive, and then be extremely positive. You will realise that life becomes easy when you face situations with a smile. When you drive in a sad, dejected mood, an accident can happen easily, because you are more disconnected with the world. But you will drive better if you are in a happy, jolly, and cheerful mood.

Also, in office, your performance will be better if you are happy. Give a soft smile to people around, and you will see that makes a big difference and gives out a better message. It opens up people's minds and hearts. Try sending out a lovely smile to people today. It will make life better and give you the strength to deal with the world.

A child is happy because he always lives in the present moment. The past is history, the future is a mystery, so enjoy the present, which is a gift. When you are ill, you get better faster if your doctor is a cheerful and happy person. Tell children and sick people that they have to smile five times every hour, and see how soon they get better.

Ensure that depressed people are taken to a better, natural environment, where it is easy to transform them. Give them a supportive environment. It is like giving them a dose of programming, just like you do with a computer. I have seen severe cases of depression change, especially if they have expressed a desire to get okay and move on.

Then, they are able to get rid of their negativity.

Usually, negative people don't find any reason to wake up or smile and find it difficult to face the world. They prefer being in a dark room and sleeping all the time. But if they have that impetus to change, they can be helped to do so. I have seen this work with young people. Their anger and pain disappears.

Analyse why people have insecurities. Sometimes, we need to introspect. Write down what you want in life and from life. What kind of life do you want to lead? Then jot down five points on how you think you can procure the lifestyle or goal you have in mind. If someone writes they want to be peaceful, then understand that they have to be healthy, get rid of their anger, earn money, look after their family, and take care of their responsibilities.

If you don't do any of these things, you are not being serious about your intentions. It means you are just talking. First make up your mind what you want and then work on your insecurities. Recognise your purpose and remove obstacles by thinking positive and eating healthy.

Greet everyone with a smile. This helps to create a great life. Try it within your family. Smile at each other today and encourage each other to smile. You have to condition yourself to do it.

Doctors who smile and ask their patients to smile have a positive effect on them. When doctors record your blood pressure and your sugar levels, they should also ask you how many times do you smile.

Let them write a prescription for you to smile a thousand times every day.

The Law of Attraction

Dr Kaity Cama

This timeless and eternal universal law is linked with our desires, with our thoughts, our emotions, with positivism and with memories relating to past actions (karma).

The Law of Attraction, by itself, is cause and effect, meaning that whatever we put out as thoughts and words and actions comes back into our lives. When used deliberately the Law of Attraction brings forth that which we send out, if it is aligned with spiritual precepts. We have all heard it said by great seers and sages and prophets that what we sow is what we reap. What goes around must come around back to us.

The Law of Attraction is an electro-magnetic force which is timeless and eternal, and it is always in motion in the entire universe, including the planets and stars. In simple language, it is simply cause and effect. Let us look at a simple analogy: if we were driving and just drive on and on without really knowing the route, we would eventually reach some place or the other, but it may not necessarily be the place we really wished to be at. If we discover the route we wish to take before embarking on the trip, it would save us time, energy and frustration. So also with the Law of Attraction—if we learn how to attract to us that which we desire, the results would be certain and fulfilling.

The first and most important thing we need to know is that our desires must be aligned with spiritual precepts, and that which we wish to attract into our lives must be of benefit to us as well as to others. Good thoughts, good words and good deeds allow us to get the assistance of all nature's forces. These forces are available to all of us who turn to them. We, as spiritual beings, are in essence electromagnetic vibrations of different frequencies, depending upon our thoughts, words and deeds.

Purity in these raises our vibratory frequency closer and closer to that of expanded awareness and helps us achieve all our constructive goals, harnessing the Law of Attraction.

If we have a goal, say, of getting a billion dollars, and our intention is to simply hoard the money, we will not achieve that goal. If our goal is to get the money to benefit us, our family, and others in some way, then we will achieve that goal.

Another important factor in harnessing the Law of Attraction is our choice of thoughts and emotions. To make a wish for something or to have a desire for something, and then to wonder whether it will work, or how long it will take, are barriers.

The frequency of such non-positive thoughts and emotions offers a resistance to the manifestation of our desires. So, first and foremost, we have to make sure that our desire is clean, honest, upright, constructive, harming no one but benefitting us and all concerned. The second point to remember is to be absolutely positive that what we have put into motion will manifest in the world on earth. These two factors are really important to remember and we need to watch out for the choices we make concerning our thoughts.

Thought is a very powerful vibratory force which, if it were to be of a non-constructive frequency, can backfire severely on us. For example, if we want to give someone a headache—a very simple example—that person will not get a headache, but we will begin to get a massive headache. We just cannot wish harm to another through thoughts without it backfiring on us.

There are two reasons why the Law of Attraction does not work for most people. One reason is that their desire is not in accord with universal and spiritual truths. The other reason is that they put up barriers by desiring something truly good and then not having the faith that it will come to them.

Those who put spirituality in motion in their lives find it a simple matter to harness the Law of Attraction—and get results to their satisfaction.

FORGIVENESS

Forgiveness is Divine

Maulana Wahiduddin Khan

What is forgiveness? Forgiveness means to grant pardon for a person's mistake or wrongdoing and not hold resentment against him or her.

For example, suppose that you are walking on the street and someone hits you with his bicycle. Then he alights from the bicycle and says: "I am very sorry, please forgive me." You don't become angry or show reaction; rather you say, "It is okay." This, on your part, is forgiveness.

Our life is full of such incidents. Every day, you face experiences of this kind. If you react and try to punish the guilty, then that will go against the spirit of forgiveness. But, if you save yourself from provocation and instead of retaliating, you remain patient and maintain calmness, then that is in keeping with the spirit of forgiveness.

It seems that forgiveness is for the other person, but in

reality it helps one's own self. Forgiveness is a great moment for your personality development. Every act of forgiveness enhances the process of your self-development. If someone offends you, it gives you a great opportunity. If you forgive at that moment, it means that you availed that opportunity. If you fail to forgive, it means you have lost a golden chance for your own development.

Forgiveness is like a strategy for buying time. When you forgive a person, you avail that time for your own development rather than losing it by abusing him. When someone offends you, and you become angry, then you lose this moment. However, if you refrain from reacting, it is bound to take you to a higher level of thinking.

If before the cycle hit you, you had a dull mind, after the accident you will emerge energised. One common belief is that those who suffer in life, emerge as super achievers later, while those who were born with a silver spoon in their mouth and went through a smooth ride in their life failed to perform any creative work.

Everyone is member of a society, large or small. The greatest identity of a person is for him to live in society as a giver member. Giving does not only mean giving something to people in terms of money. Forgiving others is also a way of giving.

Forgiveness is a very noble form of charity. The culture of forgiveness promotes positive values and constructive behaviour in society. Forgiveness means giving without taking, and giving without taking is the highest human virtue. Although forgiveness comes from the heart, it has a great external result.

Forgiveness is a great tool of cultural reform. Someone has rightly said: 'Change yourself, and you will be able to change the world.' Adopt the culture of forgiveness and you will be able to change the character of all fellow-beings.

Forgiveness is directed at others, but at first, it is for one's own self. The habit of forgiving makes one live with a peaceful mind. And, a peaceful mind is the source of all kinds of good. It gives one good health, a loving heart and friendly behaviour.

Forgiveness is of a divine character. God always forgives people for their wrongdoing. One who adopts forgiveness has adopted a divine attribute, the highest quality to which a human being can aspire.

Forgiveness: A Sweet Gift for Ourselves and Others

Dr Kaity Cama

We hear a lot about how we must forgive others, and deep within us we know it is important to forgive. We ask God to "forgive us our trespasses as we forgive others", but do we really forgive? And do we really know why it is so necessary to forgive?

Forgiveness takes us out of a karmic cycle which could go on and on otherwise. How does forgiveness get us out of a karmic cycle?

Let us think of someone who has knowingly or unknowingly hurt or harmed us in some way. The memory of that hurt usually stays with us, yes? And what does that memory do? It creates within our physical body vibrations which are incompatible with our well-being. The more we think of that incident or hurt, the longer do the vibrations stay, causing our physical body damage in the long run.

Our physical body is a spiritual gift, to be honoured and respected by us. But that is only part of the story. When we feel hurt, angry or carry negative feelings, we initiate a karmic cycle which poses a barrier between us and any form of true joy.

When the overall purpose of the soul on earth is to consciously urge the personality to recognise the oneness of all creation, a non-forgiving attitude literally pushes us away from our own peace of mind.

Judgement by itself is a habit of the ego and intellect, whereby we tend to label others: "Oh, he is not worthy of my friendship," or "She is too critical, I cannot have any conversation with her," are statements we often hear. So, the personality judges and is analytical—granted that in a worldly sense, some judgement may be necessary for the everyday person. But to carry a non-forgiving attitude may create bitter thoughts, which stay with us and against which we measure someone else's behaviour and words, thereby perhaps losing a friend before even making one.

To forgive is one of the sweetest gifts we can give to our self and to another. When we truly forgive, we actually have a little trouble remembering the unpleasant incident, and more often than not, we actually forget it. "Forgive and forget" is true forgiveness.

When we give a gift to someone with no motive other than just giving, we actually forget that we have given, and months later perhaps that individual may bring it up casually in a conversation saying how much he/she had liked it, and we feel a bit bewildered, because we have forgotten that we had given.

So also with forgiveness. We forgive and forget. This lets down the barriers which we create by nursing the memory of a hurt feeling. This allows us to move on. This also prevents a 'bad karma' cycle to begin. In addition, we become lighter and happier.

Imagine what would happen if day in and day out we carried hundreds of kilos on our head and shoulders. We wouldn't do this willingly, would we? Then why do we carry, of our own free will, those hundreds of kilos burden of emotional hurt? We need to shrug off this burden, and heartfelt forgiveness is the easiest and surest way.

Forgive and forget is the spiritual nectar that makes us respect ourselves and gain forgiveness for all our errors too. We can forgive mentally, visualising the other person. We can also ask another person mentally to forgive us if we have knowingly or unknowingly hurt that individual's feelings. We can do this with individuals who are living, and we can also do this with individuals who have departed this earth.

Just as it takes two to tango, so also any unpleasant incident which leaves a hurt feeling involves two or more people. Is it vaguely possible that the other individual felt in some way threatened, irritated or even angered by our own words or deeds?

Possible, isn't it?

So, when mentally forgiving the other individual, we can request him/her to please forgive us too. This is actually a very cleansing practice and peels off at least one layer of karmic burden from our soul.

Worth it, don't you think so?

The Healing Power of Forgiveness

Oswald Pereira

All faiths worldwide recommend it. There's universal agreement among religious leaders about its benefits. Every *avatar* of the Supreme Being and all His prophets have preached it. It's a prayer often recited by devotees in places of worship. And non-believers, too, are convinced of its great value.

Doctors tell patients about its health benefits. Old and New Age gurus will break bread to celebrate its virtues. Pranic healers and Reiki masters consider it a powerful healing tool. Forgiveness is not as sublime as love, but it's a divine virtue, without necessarily being godly.

The Oxford English Dictionary defines forgiveness thus: "To grant free pardon and to give up all claim on account of an offence or debt."

But forgiveness is much more than that. Cynics see the

act of forgiving as being one of weakness, resorted to by the meek and the cowardly. The more enlightened say only the strong are capable of it, as did Mahatma Gandhi. He said, "The weak can never forgive. Forgiveness is the attribute of the strong." Pure happiness is achieved because when you forgive a person who has done you harm, you detoxify yourself of all negative energy, free your mind, and purify your soul and body. Perhaps that's why Martin Luther said, "Forgiveness is pure happiness."

Studies at the University of Wisconsin found the more forgiving people were, the less they suffered from a wide range of illnesses. The benefits included improved functioning of their cardiovascular and nervous systems. Anger and resentment towards our so-called oppressors will bring us nothing but trouble and unhappiness. "If you do not forgive, you will continue to think of the offender and the unpleasant event," said pranic healing master Choa Kok Sui. "By forgiving and blessing, you achieve inner peace and freedom."

Those who follow Vedantic tradition pray to God to grant happiness even to their enemies. They pray to Providence not only for their well-being, but also for the prosperity of their adversaries. Vedantic wisdom believes in a prenatal harmony, a link and celestial communion among all souls. Hence, when you hate another person, you only hate yourself, as all souls are linked.

"How often do you forgive one person? Up to seven times?" Jesus Christ was asked by his disciple, Peter. Jesus replied: "I do not say to you, up to seven times, but up to seventy times seven." Jesus even asked God to forgive those who had crucified him: "Father, forgive them, for they know not what they do."

In The Lord's Prayer, Christians pray: "And forgive us our sins as we forgive those who sin against us." The message is clear: Only when you forgive others will you, too, be forgiven.

Allah is 'Most Forgiving'. Prophet Muhammad forgave people for their ignorance and was ever ready to forgive his enemies. By being unforgiving, we keep creating an identity around our pain, and that is what is reborn, Buddhists believe.

In Jainism, forgiveness is propounded as one of the main virtues to be cultivated by the faithful. Supreme forgiveness forms part of one of the ten characteristics of dharma in Jainism.

"Always forgive your enemies—nothing annoys them as much," said Oscar Wilde. It's an interesting thing to say, but taking the tongue-in-cheek remark seriously might dilute the impact and power of forgiveness.

Forgiveness has great power. It is a glorious and selfless act that could radically transform the lives of both the forgiver and the forgiven—for the better.

Forgive to Take Away the Hurt

Smita Jayakar

To forgive someone and to ask for forgiveness are the most important aspects for developing relationships and your spiritual growth. It is not just saying the words 'I am sorry' or 'I have forgiven you.' It is an emotion that should be felt deep within you, and when real forgiveness happens, you move a step further in your relationships and spiritual growth.

Lord Krishna in the *Bhagavad Gita* describes one of the qualities of a devotee as a person with a forgiving nature. Forgiveness is a quality with the power to heal an event of pain, hurt or injury. This quality is there in all of us, but we tend to push it under the carpet. Most often, it is our ego that buries this quality somewhere deep inside us.

We do not realise that by forgiving someone genuinely, we heal ourselves and lessen our karma baggage. It not only takes away the hurt and the pain caused to us by the other, but it extinguishes the past injury. It ceases to obstruct our spiritual growth, and accelerates a new beginning with that person. It washes away the negativity within us, which would otherwise eat into our vitals and affect our thinking process.

Hoo pono pono meditation is one of the best techniques used for forgiveness. It just includes four sentences: a) I am sorry b) Please forgive me c) I love you d) I thank you. You do not have to say this to the person directly. It is like a mantra, which could completely change our perception of what has been and hence what will be. By forgiving, you are not giving in, but letting go of negative emotions.

By being angry, we invite the faults of others upon ourselves. By imbibing this quality of forgiveness, we learn to see others who hurt us with new eyes. We may not immediately, or always, attain the ultimate stage of forgiveness, but at least it will start the process. But if you are willing to let go of your baggage, keep practising forgiveness as it sets in motion and triggers a change in the brain for the better.

Surprisingly, people who are forgiven may never even realise or recall that they had wronged us. In fact, for them our behaviour may appear rather strange. They may never know we have forgiven them. And they need not even know because it is not for them alone that you have done it, but for your own growth. Forgiveness is not a favour to others but to yourself.

Forgiveness is the quality of the 'Creator'—then why should the 'Created' have any other quality—and if one does, one requires to rethink.

The image of a forgiving God is best epitomised by the divine words, "Father, forgive them for they know not what they do."

I Forgave and Was Free

Chana Meddin

As a young girl, I was assaulted by someone who stole my childhood, my innocence, my inner smile. Too young to have learnt to hate, I only felt broken. It wasn't until I became an adult that I learnt the heat of anger and thoughts of revenge.

Like the *Titanic*, the shipwreck, the trauma and pain deep within was left to rust in a sea of dark consciousness, while the vicissitudes of life's tides eventually covered up sacred spaces that were sacred no more.

Forgiveness never entered my mind. But I knew anger had to leave it. How? I wanted to go home. To God. I felt inexorably drawn to eastern mysticism in a desperate search to find that painless place described in the *Upanishads, Bhagavad Gita*, and in mystic poetry. Only a true master could guide me safely into the spiritual realms within.

If the childhood experience gifted me anything, it sanctified my heart and soul with an undying flame to know God and experience inner peace, forgiveness, and letting go that I may dwell forever in that painless place.

The quest to find a true spiritual master consumed me. I discovered and followed many a fake guru for many wasted years. Eventually, jaded and cynical, I gave up and looked to nature, to wilderness and wildlife. I also became a vegetarian.

Despite the march of time, my wings remained broken.

What would it take for me to fly?

Over the years, as dawn deepened into the warmer hues of dusk, I took *Naam Dan* from Sant Rajinder Singh Ji Maharaj in one last, reluctant attempt, to fly within.

In the modest hall where he gives *satsang* at the North American headquarters for the Science of Spirituality, I sat near the front row exactly an hour before his arrival, awaiting my first glimpse of the living master. Had I, at long last, found a true guru or was this another wrong turn in the road?

I sat bewildered on the bench where I had been placed by an usher, and for the first time ever, something felt right.

One hour before Sant Rajinder Singh was scheduled to arrive, the gathering *sangat* quietly seated themselves in silent meditation. I followed their example.

I was unexpectedly enveloped by a love so intense it

was unlike anything I had ever experienced before on earth! I did not want it to end.

Before physically entering the hall, Master began pouring forth so much intoxicating love that I became a child once again. O God, what was happening? Had I lost it? Tears gushed uncontrollably from my eyes and down my cheeks, as I fell into His embrace within, with overwhelming gratitude.

Master showed me that this man I hated, had himself once been an innocent child like me. He too was some mother's precious son, someone's kid brother, playful cousin, an uncle's little nephew, a toddler, a child, and somehow I was shown how one like him could have been my very own. That we are born of love and for this man to have hurt me only revealed that he, too, had been hurt himself—so deeply wounded was he that he began wounding others.

I no longer saw inside that hurt, broken child an unconscionably cruel man but a soul—a soul like me. Duality vanished. Hatred is learnt. And in Master's grace, I discovered that what this man had so cruelly done to me had also been visited upon him! My heart burst with empathy for this man, no longer a monster but a man who had once also been an innocent child, no different than me. Master revealed this crime was not his true nature, not his identity, nor was my hatred of him mine.

For the first time in my life, I felt this man's agony and

his shame, far worse than I felt my own, and herein Master flooded my heart and soul like a cosmic fire hose with such divine love and mercy that I not only forgave this man, but became capable of loving him, grieving for all the sorrows he himself had borne, alone, throughout his terrible life.

My friend and the usher were concerned that I would not be able to stand up once Master physically entered the hall, for I was being transformed from within! I struggled to open my eyes, resembling a zombie having just been pulled from a torrential mudslide. Trembling, sobbing convulsively, my friend and the kind usher tenderly helped me to my feet, leaning not on my cane, for it had become useless—but on them...as the doors at the rear of the hall opened!

I was still shaking uncontrollably when the usher gently turned me to face the Master for the first time. Maharaj ji gently patted my quivering arm, patting so tenderly it felt unbearable, the master alchemist transforming me into his self-same love, until my arm stopped trembling beneath his silken touch. Gazing directly into my eyes, he poured forth bliss and all else ceased to exist.

Months passed. I meditated and attended weekly *satsang*, reliving as many details of meeting Master as possible, until one day, I had to do it.

I picked up the phone. Don't ask me how, for I could not tell you, but I found this man's phone number. He had become an old man and I knew nothing about him, but found his number and dialled it shakily.

"Hello?" answered an unsure, trembling voice. I did not know he had cancer and was very ill.

I told him my name.

"Do you remember me?" I asked.

"Of course I do," he replied, "Why are you calling?"

"I forgive you."

Silence. Long silence. We remained connected on the phone, neither knowing quite what to say, only that more remained for us to become whole again.

"How could you?" he asked.

"I could not," I replied truthfully. "But my spiritual teacher, Sant Rajinder Singh, gave me forgiveness with which to forgive you. So now I have."

An even longer silence followed...both of us willing to endure sacred space for that unimaginable opportunity to actually heal wounds, still apparently haunting him more than they had me.

He spoke these words: "Will you please tell this Rajinder Singh 'thank you' for me?"

"I will," I whispered. "I will."

"Thank you," he said.

"I love you," I said.

"I love you too," he said.

GOD & US

Who is Bhagawan?

Srila Bhakti Ballabh Tirtha Goswami Maharaj

He who possesses *bhaga* is *Bhagawan*. Bhaga means majesty (*aishwarya*) or potency (*shakti*). Therefore, Bhagawan is He who possesses majesty and potency. The word Bhagawan does not specifically define the type of potency or energy involved.

Bhagawan is the Omnipotent one, as per *Vishnu Purana* (6.5.74): 'One who possesses all majesty or wealth, all potency or strength, all fame, all beauty, all knowledge and all renunciation is known as Bhagawan.'

The fact that Bhagawan possesses all beauty implies that He is beautiful; therefore, He must possess form. However, in saying that He must possess form, we should not attempt to confine Him by the perishable limits of length, breadth and height.

In certain texts, it is stated that Bhagawan does not

have limbs, yet He moves. He can see without eyes, He can hear without ears. The meaning of these apparently contradictory statements is that Bhagawan does not have material form like ours, which is made up of material elements. On the contrary, He has a transcendental spiritual form.

Now, if we admit to existence of Bhagawan, we also have to admit to existence of His eneregy or *shakti*. We cannot admit existence of Bhagawan without *shakti*. Even though Bhagawan is Omnipotent, there are three predominating *shaktis* known respectively as internal potency (*chit-shakti*), the external potency (*maya shakti*) and poised in between these two are His manifested living beings known as *tattastha* or *jiva shakti*. The *shakti* that takes us to the heart of Bhagawan is known as *Antaranga shakti* (internal potency).

The *shakti* which overwhelms and enchants us with His external features, taking us away from Bhagawan, is known as *Bahiranga shakti* (external potency). The internal potency takes us towards, and the external potency takes us away from Bhagawan. The internal potency performs the unalloyed service of Bhagawan; thus it is referred to by the term 'bhakta' (devotee). *Bhakta* and Bhagawan are one non-dual substance. That one substance is composed of two moods or aspects: the predominating and the predominated, the enjoyer and the enjoyed, the served and the servitor, the object of worship and the worshipper.

Since Bhagawan is beyond our limited intellect, we cannot know Him by virtue of our merit alone. If that were so, then the very logic of Sri Bhagawan being all-opulent Supreme Lord, Omnipotent and Infinite, becomes negated. The only way of knowing Bhagawan is by the desire of Bhagawan Himself. To act according to the desire of Bhagawan is to have *preeti* (affection), or *bhakti*.

How are we to know those rules laid down in the scriptures that are dear to Bhagawan? The answer to this is, we must seek the company of devotees and take the shelter of a pure devotee of Bhagawan.

There are two types of bhakti—*vaidhi bhakti* and *raganuga bhakti*. The first is the trodden path of scriptural rules and regulations, and the second is the blazing fire of transcendental love and passion. Bhagawan can only be caught by *raganuga bhakti*. For example, Sri Nanda Maharaj and Mother Yashoda have trapped the Infinite with their pure love. If one could even reach the doors of such a devotee, would there be any doubt that he or she would definitely have *darshan* of Bhagawan? Please understand that the devotee of Bhagawan always desires to please Bhagawan.

Then again Bhagawan wants the devotee to be happy. If one loves the devotee, then that person captures Bhagawan. That is why those who love and serve Bhagawan's devotee can easily win the blessings of Bhagawan's grace.

It is not difficult to love Bhagawan. Knowledge, wealth, beauty, power, are not required in this love. As per *Sreemad Bhagawatam* (1.8.26), 'Those who are intoxicated with their birth (social status), wealth, learning and beauty are incapable of uttering the name of Krishna, which can be taken by those who are bereft of all material assets.'

If all the pride in the world should occupy all the space in my heart, if I expend all my energies to chase wealth, sex and power, then how can Sri Bhagawan find a place in such a heart? Although a welcome sign hangs at the gate, when the inside of the house is cluttered up with so much rubbish, the invited guest turns away, being unable to find a place to sit.

In like manner, it is no use to externally extend a welcome to Bhagawan if the inside is clogged up with unwanted desires. Bhagawan may very well come, but He will go away without finding a place to sit.

Where is God?

Swamini Atmaprajnananda Saraswati

A common question is: 'Where is God?'

When one asks where is God, one has already given him/ her a place/location, and has concluded that others around that area are not God ... the plants/animals are not God, the inanimate things immediately around are not God, and of course, the person asking the question definitely does not consider himself/herself to be God. People also look up while taking the name of God, implying that He is up there, and never down, and certainly not around.

One Russian astronaut even went to space and concluded that there is no God in space. Way back on April 12, 1961, aboard his Vostok 3KA-2 spacecraft, Yuri Alekseyevich Gagarin became the first human in outer space and the first to orbit the earth. It was reported that he said after exiting the earth's orbit, "I don't see any God up here." Someone wryly quipped then, "If a cosmonaut wants to see God, all he has to do is exit his craft and take off his space suit. He will meet God."

If you say you have not seen Amitabh Bachchan, it is believable, because everybody knows what he looks like. When you say you have not seen God, the next question should be, "Which God are you talking about?" People have ideas about what God looks like, or should look like, which is mostly the *dhyäna-murti*s described in scriptures for meditation or visualisation. To think that God is restricted to a particular form is actually a state of naiveté or innocence.

In all cultures that accept the presence of God, the concept is: 'God in his heaven created this world'. In Hindu culture as well, some call it *Vaikuntha*, some call it *Kailäsa*. God is given a *näma-rupa*, as well as a place. So, God is regarded as an entity different from the world.

What is the fallacy in this statement or belief? A God belonging to a place cannot be *sarvavyäpi* or omnipresent, *anantam* or limitless. He is limited by the *jagat* he created. Now, how do we break the riddle?

The *Upanishads* present God as the Maker and the Material Cause, and thereby answer all questions. The question as to where God is, is not answered, unless we ponder the question the way the *Upanishads* do.

When we enquire into creation and its cause, we

should not confine ourselves to a part, but should look at the whole. We cannot get right answers if we ask wrong questions, because the answer we get is always in keeping with the question, and so, if we ask the right question, there will be a right answer.

In Advaita Vedanta, the phrase *abhinna nimitta-upädäna-kärana* means *Brahman* is the intelligent as well as the material cause of this manifest universe. When we enquire into the nature of the cause for creation, we find there must be two causes for any creation—the Maker and the Material.

The Maker, the one who is responsible for Creation, is called the efficient cause (intelligent cause) or *nimitta-kärana*. Secondly, there must be some material out of which any given thing can be created. For creating a pot, for example, there must be a potter, the efficient or intelligent cause. There should also be some raw material, such as clay or copper or brass out of which the pot is to be made.

Taittiriya Upanishad presents *Brahman* as the *nimitta-kärana* of this *jagat— 'so'kämayata. bahu syäm prajäyeyeti. Sa tapo'tapyata. sa tapastaptvä. Idagm sarvam asrjata. Yadidam kinca. Tat srstvä. Ttad evänupravisat. (Tai.Up. - II.6)*

Now, with reference to the creation of the universe, if Isvara, the Lord, is the Maker and the Efficient Cause, the next question is: What is the material out of which God created this world? When we are enquiring into the nature of the cause of Creation, we must take into account the material also. Creation had baffled the *rishis*, and it continues to baffle the scientists and the astrophysicists till date.

Where did the Lord find the material? Here, we must also bear in mind that both space and time are part of Creation, and so before Creation, there is nothing outside Creation because 'outside' is a concept in space which is not yet created.

Therefore, there is nothing outside the Lord before Creation, and so, the Material should be within the Lord. That is why He is called the Lord. Therefore, not only is the Lord the Maker, but He is the Material too.

The same Brahmänandavalli of *Taittiriya* gives a model of this Creation, stating, '*Tasmät vä etasmät ätmana äkäsah sambhutah (Tai. Up. II.1)* meaning—'from that Lord that is (non-different from) this self, *äkäsa,* the space, was born. From the space was born air, from air was born fire, from fire water, from water earth was born. Other Upanisads—*Mundaka* and *Chändogya*—give this model of five/three elements, and their combinations.

While explaining how the Maker and the Material of this Universe are one, *Mundakopanishad* gives us the illustration of a spider: *Yathä ürnanabhih srjate grhnateca*—'just as a spider creates (a web) and withdraws it too'.

The spider is the efficient cause of the web, because

it has the intelligence and the skill to create the web. It chooses the right place for the web, where it would not be swept away by the woman of the house and where it can get its prey.

This shows that the spider has intelligence. And the material for the web is the secretion of a gland which it finds within itself.

So too, the Lord projects this creation and withdraws it unto Himself at the time of dissolution.

How Did We Happen?

Om Swami

Even if someone gave you the most accurate answer to the question, 'How did we happen?', you might still not accept it because there's often no way of verifying its validity. Everything on our origin, death and afterlife is a theory, some theories sounding more plausible than others.

There is no heaven or hell. There is no supernatural creator. There is no universal purpose applicable to all individuals. There may even be no individual purpose because the quest for purpose is a craving of the conscious mind. Why does a sense of purpose disappear in sleep, or when one is unconscious, or in an infant? As we grow, a sense of ego, of individuality, makes us feel that life can't be meaningless. This notion of meaning is simply a pointless ramble of the conscious mind.

The brutal truth is that every being, every single entity,

if anything, is merely an insignificant, dispensable and disposable aspect of Nature, whose self-fulfilling purpose is to sustain itself.

The theory of evolution is the most sensible response to the question of how did we happen. But, it doesn't give us the complete picture either, because it misses out on the basis of evolution—it tries to explain how we happened and not why. Why do we even take birth, or why do we evolve? We do so, because in my view, Nature recycles.

If you observe closely, everything in Nature is recycled. Absolutely everything. The five elements of earth, water, fire, air, ether, and the innumerable compounds thereof, all entities—living or non-living, animate or inanimate—they are all subject to recycling. Everything, including our body is salvaged by Nature. Our consciousness too finds a new home after death. Nature's only goal is survival; and it accomplishes it through the eternal cycle of transformation. That's how and why we happen(ed).

The other day, I was walking back to my hut at night and a dog was walking in front. Due to the heavy rains, all sorts of creatures had appeared out of nowhere (talk about creation). Inadvertently, the dog stepped on a snail. I sat down and flashed my light on the snail. It had turned into pulp and was crushed under the weight of its own shell. The dog kept looking at me lovingly, completely oblivious to the life it just took.

I sat there for a wee bit more and tiny insects began gathering up on the dead snail. In no time, bigger insects made way into the equation and started devouring their meal. I carried on observing and it began drizzling. Meanwhile, the struggle between the insects continued—each wanting more. Soon, the soft showers turned into torrents and the smaller insects ran for their lives. A few minutes later, the larger ones fled as well under the heavy rain and left in front of me was a gored snail. The dog too had taken shelter under the nearby roof. The rain stopped. I waited a bit more and the insects started to return.

I looked at the dark sky, at the quiet mountains, at the roaring river. What a magnificent play of nature, I thought. Sunlight during the day had given birth to billions of tiny creatures and a downpour of a few minutes had wiped them off the face of the earth. Countless crawl out from the womb of Mother Nature and countless merge back. Every moment. I prayed for the sentient beings and went back to my hut.

I've observed ants, insects, fish, snakes, scorpions, wolves, deer, bears, boar, baboons, monkeys and humans. There's no difference. When it comes to Nature, when it comes to the inexplicable essence I call God, there's absolutely no difference whether a dog steps on a snail or an elephant on a man. Whether a flood destroys a thousand sheep or a tsunami, a thousand humans, Nature makes no distinction. Human sense of superiority or a conceited notion of being special is merely an arrogant view. It shows a lack of understanding; it demonstrates an absence of compassion.

In the words of the celebrated Chinese thinker and philosopher, Wu Hsin:

How many of your questions
Have been answered,
But still
You don't have the answer?
Is it possible that
The answer isn't
Found in more questions?
Is it possible that
The answer isn't
Found in more concepts,
More thoughts?
Is it possible that
The answer is
Revealed in their very absence?
(Roy Melvyn, *The Lost Writings of Wu Hsin*)

Somehow, you believe that every question ought to have an answer. An absolute answer, at that. It's a vain and a childish view. The books of the wise ones contain no absolute answers.

Why is the universe infinite? What will you say when

your child asks you why was I born to you, O mother? I can give you the answers but they won't lead you to your truth. Rather than answering your questions, let's question your answers. Your questions are not the problem. Your answers are.

How I Fell In and Out With God

Oswald Pereira

When we were children, we were told that God is present everywhere. So, as a kid I saw God's hand in nature and in everything small and beautiful.

My favourite God-creation was a butterfly. I used to creep up towards a butterfly and gently holding it, marvel at its colours and beauty. When I released it, it would flutter its wings and return to rest on a sunflower in the garden of our home.

In school, I always scored the highest marks in religion, winning the first prize that consisted of small, hardbound books on God and religion. My peers who were happier eyeing the 'birds' in class gave me up for a lost case and concluded that I would join a seminary after school.

Then one day, my religion teacher declared in catechism class with a startling finality that the only way to

Heaven is through 'our God'. I should have jumped at that announcement, happy that he had assured us all a place in Heaven, especially the religious me.

But I was quite disturbed by his declaration and timidly asked him, "What happens to those from other faiths?"

He was aghast by my question and scolded me, saying, "Don't you know, we are God's chosen people."

Period. End of catechism class.

But that was also the end of my unstinting belief in God. To me, God suddenly became unjust to have 'chosen' only part of his people to go to Heaven. As I began to play truant with God, my scores in religion fell. By the time I reached the 11th standard, I had joined the league of non-believers.

On one of the bleakest days of my life, my mother was summoned by the school principal because my hair was long and I had made a puff—in the Dev Anand-Elvis Presley style. The principal, a religious person, had flattened my puff that I used to so painstakingly create and made me kneel down for looking like a 'Roadside Romeo'. That humiliating experience, indeed, was a nail in the coffin of my belief in religion and God. How could a religious person behave so insensitively? I asked and fell out with religion and God.

I made my peace with God on joining the Charismatic Movement, ten years after my puff was ruffled by my school principal. It was quite evident that I was still a believer as I received the Holy Spirit's gift to pray and some power to heal. But this didn't last long as I was sucked into the world of journalism where my priorities changed—news scoops, followed by celebrations at the Bombay Press Club became a routine affair. There was clearly a mismatch between the Holy Spirit and manmade spirit.

However, there is still hope of happier days, as I recently came face-to-face with one uplifting moment. The moment has grown into seconds and the seconds into minutes. The duration of peace and joy within is slowly growing and building up. The more effort I put into the exercise, the greater the reward. There is the feel of a Supreme Being that is cleansing and energising my body, mind and spirit. This time around, I want to make the joy last, forever. Like the puff of my hair in my younger days, it's a puff of the spirit.

But the faith can only sustain if the puff grows into a mountain—and one that can't be ruffled with the fingers.

Yes, God is everywhere, with all of us, at all times. But I've learnt the hard way that He is first within you. You should not let any person or external force disturb your equation with God. And the only way to Heaven is through God—yours, mine and ours.

Take a Walk With Divinity

Reena Singh

It is not for nothing that spiritual masters, *yogacharyas*, *ayurvedacharyas* and fitness experts tell you to go take a walk as a cure for almost anything and everything.

It whittles down your fat, puts you in a happier frame of mind if you are upset; for sure, the blackest of all moods disappear as the cool breeze caresses your face as you walk.

Neural activity is heightened and brainwaves might suddenly occur while you move your limbs and eureka! you might even come up with answers to the most unsolvable riddles of your life. A walk among nature always rejuvenates and peps you up. It fills you with endorphins, those feel-good hormones that make your day go better.

It is also a completely natural activity that matches, movement for movement, an activity that our ancestors did millennia ago. Of course they did it without fancy air shoes and minus the swagger or waddle that some of us are now wont to adopt, for the simple reason that whatever the mood you might find yourself in, walking limbers you up to face your day. It pushes your circulation up, and ensures that every pore and cell of your being is oxygenated with natural *prana* flowing into your millions of *nadis* and veins.

Spiritual masters talk about nature and about the need to go walking amidst it. Buddhist monk, Thich Nhat Hanh takes walking one step further and prescribes Mindful Walking to his disciples. Some people chant as they walk, chanting the syllable of a *mantra* at every step, coordinating it with breathing in and out.

Walking is nature's superlative gift to us, besides being the best-ever aerobic activity known in nature. It uses up all your 600-plus major muscle groups, and you could burn anything from six to eight calories per minute, depending on your weight, size and pace of walking. Walking allows you to take in deep breaths naturally, and needs nothing besides early morning or evening pleasant weather that turn the simplest of all walks into a rejuvenating and health-giving free gift from nature. It increases bone density too, and is known to be the most effective flab-fighting activity that exists. There is no age limit to walking. A baby of one year learns to walk and almost everyone walks till the last days of their lives.

You have to try walking on fresh green grass early

mornings and then sit down in a park on a bench beneath a tree soaking in health-giving *prana* from the trees and leaves just a few times.

You will soon be hooked.

Healthcare workers prescribe it as routinely as they do their medicines, knowing that this one ingredient has better chances of setting you back on the road to good health, than all the medicines they have scribbled for you on your prescription sheets.

The irony is that half those ailments wouldn't have made an appearance in your body if you had done your share of daily walking as the Creator had meant it to be. That's how important walking is. The Divine gave you this gift so that you could commune with beautiful nature and breathe in the divinity that surrounds you.

Suffering is a Blessing From God

Oswald Pereira

If we take full responsibility for our actions and realise that we may, in fact, have brought suffering upon us, we will learn to bear the pain with calmness. We must realise that no suffering is permanent and the worst ultimately passes away by surrendering ourselves and our actions to God.

Our suffering stems from our ego, our lack of knowledge and attachment. Jesus Christ is an example of detachment. He surrendered his life for the sake of mankind and obeyed God, The Father, without question. Jesus also preached the futility of attachment to material possessions.

Lord Krishna's teaching of *Nishkama Karma* or desireless action, without worrying about the fruits, if put into practice will help us to deal with suffering, because then we will look upon joy and suffering, failure and success, richness and poverty with equanimity.

Our suffering will no longer seem like suffering when we submit ourselves to God's will. Muslims too believe that we will understand suffering better when we trust in God: "The *Quran* tells us that good, evil and whatever happens in this world happens by Allah's Will (*mashi'at* Allah). Only Allah knows fully His Will. We finite beings cannot grasp fully His infinite Will and Wisdom. He runs His universe the way He deems fit. The *Quran* tells us that Allah is Wise and everything that Allah does is right, just, good and fair. We must submit and surrender to His Will."

Hindus believe that "suffering is a by-product of the influence of maya." Maya isn't eliminated through our own personal effort. It ends only through God's divine power of grace. The *Upanishads* teach us that the "world of diversity and suffering is not the real world and that our apparent, suffering self is not real either."

I think that we should never pass the blame for our suffering on the devil or Satan. If we suffer, we should blame ourselves, because both God and Satan are within us. Who wins, God or Satan, is entirely in our hands.

Yes, God is both the ruler and the facilitator, but as is often said, "God helps those who help themselves."

There's a lot to learn on suffering from various faiths. If all religions come together and we have multi-faith prayer meetings, it may help us in taking a new look at our sufferings.

Imagine the infinite divine energy and goodness that will pour out of such meetings.

Suffering may not be eliminated, but we would have learnt to deal with it as one world community belonging to the One and Only God.

If suffering leads to unity of mankind, we will realise that suffering is a blessing from God.

Music and Divinity

Arjun Pereira

Singing and music take you to higher states of awareness. The creativity that you express in your singing and music is a manifestation of divine energy, which inspires you to express words and feelings in extraordinary ways.

The divine communicates with everyone regardless of caste, colour and creed. Similarly, music communicates with everyone irrespective of human made distinctions. Music is in the 16th realm, the highest level of consciousness, when you sing and play with gratitude to the Supreme Being.

When music and singing are used to go against the divine, and worship of the materialistic or to express self-destructive thoughts, this is when it leads to the inevitable collapse of the individual. Myriads of singers and musicians fall prey to alcoholism, promiscuity, drugs, giant ego and other manifestations that are outside the divine characteristics of music.

Many primitive tribes recognised the importance of singing and music as they would evoke the Creator's blessings and healing touches by the communication of melodious music.

Singing and music is not only for big audiences or to get standing ovations. This art form is also for yourself to express your own love for the divine and your environment. Recently, a scientific study conclusively proved that trees and plants respond to music as much as humans, as they are high survival creations of the Supreme Being.

We instinctively admire singers and musicians as they connect us to the divine in a subtle if not direct fashion. The ones who are truly connected to the divine give us hope and inspiration, sometimes when we require it the most.

Musicians are at a level above ordinary men by their connection with the divine. One must enable them to create as much as they can and not interfere with their creative efforts. In a society in which everyone is truly connected to the divine through singing, music, or otherwise, there will be no tensions, as everyone will be serene when they realise that they are a manifestation of purity and the highest consciousness.

In an article in the *National Geographic* magazine, biomusicologists argue that not only are the sounds of some animals pleasing, but they are also composed of the same musical language that humans use. Whales, for example, use many of the musical concepts found in human music, including similar rhythms, phrase lengths, and song structure.

These similarities, the writers maintain, "prove that these marine mammals are inveterate composers." Bird songs follow rhythmic patterns and pitches that are in tune with human music. Birds not only create vocal sound, some also add a percussion instrument to their songs, the writers affirm.

Another sound that is of vital importance in singing and music is *Om*, the primordial sound of this Universe. Chanting *Om* frequently helps one to sing and play an instrument better as well as to listen better. *Om* is known to be the sound that connects you to the Divine. *Om* also connects you to singing and music.

To conclude, we reach greater heights of music and singing, peaking at the highest realm when we perform with consciousness and gratitude for the Supreme Being.

God is Everywhere

Oswald Pereira

When I was a child barely three years old, before I even knew who or what God is, my mother told me God is everywhere. She didn't even tell me God exists in heaven, because that would mean explaining the meaning of heaven.

How would a child understand what heaven is? And telling a child about heaven and hell is not a wise thing to do, my mother seemed to have figured out.

I tried to tell my son when he turned three what my mother had told me.

But he asked me, "But why is God everywhere? Show me, show me, God."

I had no explanation and couldn't show him God.

So, he got busy with his toys, but said cutely, "Daddy, you don't know, no?

I smiled in reply.

"After I finish playing, tell me another nice story," he said.

I was delighted. At least, he thought the 'God Is Everywhere' concept a nice story.

Isn't it nice to know that God is everywhere? If we believe that God is everywhere, we will learn to see Him in happiness and sorrow, in good and bad, in the beautiful and the ugly, in love and hate, in friends and enemies, in war and in peace, in richness and poverty; in our heart, mind and soul.

As Lord Krishna says in the *Bhagavad Gita*, "Intelligence, knowledge, freedom from doubt and delusion, forgiveness, truthfulness, control of the senses, control of the mind, happiness and distress, birth, death, fear, fearlessness, non-violence, equanimity, satisfaction, austerity, charity, fame and infamy—all these various qualities of living beings are created by Me alone." (10.4-5)

There's God in the innocent smile of a child. God is present in a butterfly, in the smallest of living creatures, as well as in big animals. If we believe that God is everywhere, we may be blessed with the understanding about who God really is, what He really is.

Then we may not have to look for God in heaven; because we don't know where heaven is. But we do know where earth is. By believing that God is everywhere here on this earth, He becomes more understandable. When we feel God's presence around us, it follows that He is within us too. And if He is within us, He must be within people around us, because He is everywhere and in every person.

Lord Krishna says in the *Gita*, "I am the Supersoul, O Arjuna, seated in the hearts of all living entities. I am the beginning, the middle and the end of all beings." (10.20)

Borrowing from Lionel Richie's song, I just heard God ask: *"Hello, is it me you're looking for? I can see it in your eyes, I can see it in your smile, You're all I've ever wanted, and my arms are open wide, 'Cause you know just what to say And you know just what to do And I want to tell you so much, I love you."*

Beautiful God

Ismita Tandon

In prayerfulness,
In the sweet music of your many names,
I lose myself to you.
All is bare, all is beautiful.
The seed of this vast, infinite existence is you.
In your world there's no haste, no gushing waters,
No tidal waves, neither joy, nor pain.
All is still, all is grace.
The magnitude of your greatness I cannot contain.
Now I see the world from different eyes.
I see love raining from the skies.
All is coloured.
All is chaste.
All of creation is but a rendition of your unknowable, unspeakable form.